BASQUE
Cooking and Lore

BASQUE
Cooking and Lore

By
Darcy Williamson

Illustrations by Shannon Dee
and Kathleen Petersen

Cover Artwork by Larry Milligan

Cover Design by Teresa Sales

The CAXTON PRINTERS, Ltd.
Caldwell, Idaho
1993

First Printing March, 1992
Second Printing May, 1993

Library of Congress Cataloging-in-Publication Data

Williamson, Darcy.
   Basque cooking and lore / by Darcy Williamson ; illustrations by
Shannon Dee and Kathy Peterson ; cover by Larry Milligan.
      p.   cm.
   Includes bibliographical references and indexes.
   ISBN 0-87004-346-3 : $10.95
   1. Cookery, Basque.   2. Basque Americans--West (U.S.)--Folklore.
I. Title
TX723.5.B3W55   1991
641.5946'6--dc20   91-24000
                                                                         CIP
                                                                         Rev.

Lithographed and bound in the United States of America by
The CAXTON PRINTERS, Ltd.
Caldwell, ID 83605

157430

*Dedicated to the Basques of
the American West —
Past, Present, and Future*

Contents

THE BASQUES

On the shores of the Bay of Biscay, where the Pyrenees slope down to the sea, there lies a smiling land whose varied charm is made up of indented sea coast, rugged mountains and green valleys, rolling hills covered with golden gorse and forests of oak and chestnut, trout streams and maise fields, shady lanes, sun-soaked vineyards and apple orchards.

From time immemorial, this land has been inhabited by a mysterious race whom we call the Basques, but who call them-selves "Euzkaldunak" and their land "Eskual Herria" or "Euzkadi," a name which may, perhaps, be derived from the Basque word for "sun". The Basque lands consist of seven provinces, four in Spain and three in France. Politically, some Basques are Span-ish citizens, the rest French citizens, but originally, and by natural law, they are neither French nor Spanish. All are, quite simply, Basque. On the Basque Coat of Arms are emblazoned the historic crests of the seven original Basque provinces. Despite division, the enduring entity of the Basques can be found in the words "Zapiak-Bat" (The Seven are One).

The structure of the Basque language is tremendously complicated. It relates to no other know language, and researchers who have tried to translate the Basque verb say that it cannot be done.

The Basque were known as a proud and fierce race of warriors. As early as 10 B.C. they repulsed Roman Legions bent on in-vading their mountains. After the fall of the Roman Empire, they still remained uncon-quered. The Basque War Cry, the "irrintzi," has been described as beginning with a derisive laugh, then changing to a horse's shrill neigh, then to a wolf's howl, and end-ing like the expiring notes of a jackass' bray. Napoleon's soldiers who were invading Spain were said to shudder whenever they heard this "cry." The Basque, when the spirit moves him, at festive occasions still gives vent to the "old war cry."

By relating briefly the history of the primitive people of Spain and making a comparison of the languages they spoke, and the Basque language, perhaps we could form an opinion concerning who the Basques might be.

The oldest, or the first known, inhabitants of Spain were the Iberians — hence the Iberian Peninsula, which extends beyond the Pyrenees to what is now France. Then came the Celts from the north, crossing the Pyrenees and establishing themselves in various regions of Spain. These two races intermingled, and as a result, a new stock was developed, known as the Celtiberians. Next came the Phoenicians, the first civil-ized people to land in Spain; they were fol-lowed by the Greeks, who founded several cities along the Mediterranean shore.

The Carthaginians followed, conquering a large area of Spain and extending their possessions as far north as the Ebro River. They stayed a comparitively short time in Spain, for a war broke out between them and their archrivals, the Romans, who defeated them and forced them to give up their possessions in Spain. The Romans then proceeded in bringing the Iberian Peninsula under their rule. Barbarians from the north invaded Spain next and the Rom-ans were unable to offer any effective resistance.

In the early part of the fifth (5th) century, Spain was attacked by the Germanic tribes, namely the Vandals, Suevi, Alanes, etc.; they in turn were attacked by the Moors, who conquered the greatest part of the Iberian Peninsula.

During the Moorish invasion of Spain, which began in 711 A.D., the two Basque provinces, Guipuzcoa and Viscaya, were never conquered. Because of this fact, nobility was granted by the King to all in-habitants of these two provinces. In 1212, at Las Navas De Tolosa, the stain of Fun-quera was wiped out and the North of Spain was finally cleansed of the Moors. Because of their assistance in this matter, "fueros" (charters) were granted to the Basques. The Basques then exercised almost a pure form of democracy.

In the first Carlist War (1839) and the 2nd Carlist War (1876) they again fought for freedom and lost. It was at this point that the remarkable Basque culture underwent a fair degree of change, through the loss of their inherent liberties and the forced introduc-tion of the French and Spanish languages and customs. Possession of a Basque flag, whose colors are red, white and green, was forbidden by law and wearing of some of the traditional Basque colors and singing of some of the old native Basque songs were prohibited. The fueros (charters), the tradi-tional inheritance of the Basques from the Dark Ages, and the warrant of their national independence to which they clung for nearly a thousand years, and the final loss of which, when they had become a glaring anachronism, spelled the end of the inde-pendent existence.

Stripped of their liberties, the young men of "Euzkadi" began to migrate to North and South America. Before the 1936-39 Civil War in Spain, emigration from Eskual-Herria for centuries just about balanced the birth rate. It was stories of great riches and oppor-tunities of the new Americas which led them here.

The first record of the Basques in North America was when they came to California in the Gold Rush of 1849. They found little gold. From California they moved east into Nevada, Utah and Idaho and accepted any sort of honorable occupations to survive. Some of the Basques accepted jobs as sheepherders, even though most of the Basques had never herded sheep in their native land. Because they brought in fat lambs with very little herd losses, they were soon sought after by sheep raisers. Since that time their fame as sheepherders has become widely known.

The Basques were renowned as a sea-far-ing people. As early as the 12th Century their whaling and cod-fishing expeditions took them near the Newfoundland Coast. Juan Sebastian Elcano of Guetaris, another Basque, was the first sea captain to circum-navigate the globe. When Philippine sav-ages killed Magellan in 1521, Elacano, who commanded one of the five ships in Magel-lan's earthgirdling expedition, succeeded him as a leader and became the first sea captain to circumnavigate the globe.

The Basques seem ideally suited for cer-tain fast-moving kinds of sports, in which the more modern type of man rapidly burns out. The viciously fast game of jai-alai, sometimes called pelota by the Spanish, was adopted from the Basques.

Music is deeply inbred in the Basque peo-ple, they are strenuous and agile dancers.

The largest colony of Basques in the world outside of their native land is in the Boise Valley. The second largest concentra-tion is believed to be in the San Joaquin Valley of California.

The Boise Euzkaldunak still maintain, in part, the customs of competitive games and traditional dances.

The Basques are proud Americans and proud of their heritage.

Breads

Tongues are more active than brooms.

Basque Proverb

Black Olive Bread
2 loaves

5 tsp. active dry yeast
1½ tsp. sugar
1 tsp. pepper
1 cup corn flour
2½ cups whole wheat flour
1½ cups pitted and chopped brine-cured black olives
2 Tbsp. Spanish olive oil

Proof yeast with ¼ cup warm water, sugar and pepper for 10 minutes. Add corn and wheat flours, olives and olive oil. Knead dough gently on floured surface. Cover and put in warm place until double in bulk. Turn onto floured surface, cut in half and form each half into a round loaf. Place on baking sheets, dust with corn flour, cover loosely and let rise until nearly double in bulk. Slash tops with razor and bake in 400°F preheated over for 25 minutes.

Dutch Oven Baking Powder Biscuits

2 cups sifted all-purpose flour
1 Tbsp. baking powder
½ tsp. salt
¼ cup butter, softened
¾ cup milk
2 Tbsp. sugar

Sift together dry ingredients. Cut in butter. Add milk and stir quickly until dough clings together. Turn onto floured board and knead a few times. Pat or roll out to one-half thickness. Cut into rounds with floured cutter. Place rounds in buttered or greased Dutch oven. Cover. Place in hot coals, placing a few coals on lid, and bake for 15 minutes or until light brown.

Dutch Oven Cornbread

2 cups yellow cornmeal,
   pulverized in food processor until fine
1 tsp. salt
1½ cups boiling water
1½ Tbsp. Spanish olive oil
1 pkg. active dry yeast
1/3 cup lukewarm water
2 tsp. sugar
1¾ cups all-purpose flour
Olive oil

Combine 1 cup cornmeal, salt, and boiling water. Beat until smooth. Stir in olive oil, then cool to lukewarm.

In bowl, sprinkle yeast and sugar over lukewarm water. Let stand for 3 minutes, then stir. Place in warm spot for 10 minutes. Stir into cornmeal mixture. Gradually add remaining cornmeal and 1½ cups flour. Gather dough into a ball, cover with cloth, and let rise until double in bulk. Punch down and knead, working in remaining flour. Pat into a round loaf.

Coat sides and bottom of Dutch oven with olive oil. Place loaf in Dutch oven, cover, and let rise until double in bulk. Bake at 350°F for 30 to 35 minutes, or bake over hot campfire until done.

Talo
(flat cornbread)

3½ cups corn flour
1 tsp. salt
Water

Combine corn flour and salt. Slowly add tepid water until a soft dough forms. Form dough into balls the size of oranges. Let rise near heat for 1 hour.

Flatten balls into thin patties. Place on hot griddle over hot stove or camp fire. Cook each side until lightly browned.

This is often broken into milk and eaten for breakfast.

Salt-Rising Dutch Oven Bread

Liquid from Salt-Rising Starter (recipe follows)
½ cup warm water
¼ tsp. baking soda
½ cup scalded and cooled milk
1 Tbsp. melted butter
½ tsp. salt
4½ to 5½ cups hard wheat flour

Drain starter from potato into a mixing bowl and pour ½ cup warm water through potato. Discard potato. Add rinse water to starter along with baking soda, milk, butter, and salt. Mix well. Add 2 cups flour and beat smooth. Stir in remaining flour, a cup at a time, until a soft dough is formed. Sprinkle a board with flour, turn out dough and knead until smooth, but still soft.

Brush sides and bottom of Dutch oven with butter. Shape dough into a round loaf and place in Dutch oven. Let rise in warm place until double in bulk (4 to 5 hours).

Cover Dutch oven. Add a few coals on top of lid. Bake in hot coals of camp fire for 45 minutes to an hour, depending on heat. May be baked in a 375°F oven for 45 to 50 minutes.

Remove bread from pan and cool.

Salt-Rising Starter

1½ cups hot water
1 medium potato, peeled and sliced thin
2 Tbsp. yellow cornmeal
2 tsp. sugar
½ tsp. salt

Mix together ingredients and pour into 2 quart crock which has been rinsed with hot water. Cover with old blankets or towels and set beside campfire. Keep warm overnight. (Or allow to stand at 100°F for 12 to 24 hours until top is covered with one-half inch to one inch foam.)

Basque Dutch Oven Beer Bread

3 cups whole wheat flour
1½ cups white flour
½ cup white cornmeal
½ cup bran
1½ tsp. baking powder
1½ tsp. baking soda
½ cup sugar
1 12 oz. bottle dark (or stout) beer
½ cup warm water
1/3 cup vegetable oil

Dump ingredients in bowl and add one 12 oz. bottle dark (or stout) beer and ½ cup warm water. Stir in 1/3 cup vegetable oil and mix until dry ingredients are moistened. Pour batter into well-oiled Dutch oven and bake, covered, in preheated 350°F oven for 35 to 40 minutes.

Vegetables

If a man lives well, he dies well.

Basque Proverb

Asparagus Menestra
Serves 6

2 Tbsp. Spanish olive oil
½ cup chopped onion
2 oz. chorizo, cut into thin rounds
¼ cup diced salt pork
1½ Tbsp. flour
1 cup dry white wine
½ cup liquid from asparagus
2 lbs. asparagus tips

Steam asparagus tips until tender but not over-cooked. Reserve ½ cup liquid from steaming.

Heat oil in heavy skillet over moderate heat until light haze forms. Add onion, chorizo, and salt pork. When onion is translucent, add flour and stir gently. Add wine and asparagus liquid. Bring to a boil, then pour over asparagus.

Basque Potatoes
Serves 4

½ cup finely chopped onion
½ cup chopped Italian parsley
½ cup shredded carrot
2 cloves garlic, minced
2 Tbsp. Spanish olive oil
1½ cups chicken broth
4½ cups cubed potatoes (approximately 1")
Salt and pepper to taste

In skillet cook onion, parsley, carrot, and garlic in olive oil until vegetables are tender. Add broth, potatoes, salt, and pepper to taste. Cover and simmer for 10 minutes. Uncover and simmer, stirring occasionally, for 20 minutes. Garnish with additional parsley, if desired.

Berza
(cabbage with short ribs)
Serves 4

½ lb. pork short ribs
3 Tbsp. salt
1 medium head cabbage
½ cup Spanish olive oil
4 cloves garlic

Simmer ribs in large kettle in 2½ quarts boiling water to which salt has been added, for 1 hour.

Remove core from cabbage and place head in a kettle of simmering water. Separate leaves from head as they wilt. Cook, covered, 20 minutes. Drain cabbage and ribs.

In heavy Dutch oven, heat oil over medium heat. Add garlic cloves and cook until browned. Remove and discard cloves. Increase heat until light haze forms. Add well-drained cabbage and ribs and cook until cabbage begins to brown. Season to taste. with salt and pepper.

Broccoli and Roasted Peppers
Serves 5 to 6

2 large red bell peppers
1 lb. broccoli, trimmed and stems peeled
2 cloves garlic
¼ cup Spanish olive oil
Few hot red pepper flakes

Char peppers in broiler until skin blackens. Place peppers in plastic bag and allow to steam for 10 minutes. Peel, seed, and cut peppers into ¼" strips.

Soak broccoli in salted water for 10 minutes. Drain well. Steam until tender.

Crush garlic. Heat oil, garlic and hot red pepper flakes in heavy skillet over medium high heat and cook until garlic is a light brown. Discard garlic. Toss hot broccoli and peppers with oil. Serve at once.

Fresh Baby Lima Beans with Ham Hocks
Serves 4

½ lb. fresh baby lima beans
½ lb. ham hocks
Water

Cook ham hocks in water to cover for 1½ hours. Add beans, cover and simmer gently until limas are tender.

Fried Peppers
Serves 4

2 large sweet red peppers,
    seeded, roasted, and peeled
2 large green peppers,
    seeded, roasted, and peeled
2 large cloves garlic, minced
½ cup Spanish olive oil
¼ tsp. salt

Cut roasted and peeled peppers into strips. Heat oil in heavy skillet over high heat until light haze forms. Reduce heat to low. Add peppers and garlic. Fry until peppers are tender.

(Note: to roast peppers, see Roasted Red or Green Peppers in Miscellaneous section)

New Potatotes in Parsley Sauce
Serves 4

1/3 cup Spanish olive oil
6 medium new red potatoes, sliced into ½" rounds
½ cup finely chopped onions
1 tsp. finely chopped garlic
¼ cup finely chopped parsley
½ tsp. salt
¼ tsp. freshly ground pepper
1 Tbsp. white wine vinegar
1¼ cups boiling water

In heavy skillet heat olive oil over high heat until light haze forms. Add potatoes. Turn frequently with spatula and cook 10 minutes, or until they are light golden brown.

Scatter onions, garlic, parsley, salt, and pepper on top of potatoes and pour vinegar and boiling water over all. Do not stir. Shake pan back and forth for a minute or two to distribute water evenly.

Cover skillet tightly and simmer over low heat for 20 minutes. Shake skillet back and forth to prevent potatoes from sticking to bottom of pan.

Transfer potatoes to a platter. Serve cooking liquid on side.

Rice with Fresh Green Peas
Serves 4

2 Tbsp. Spanish olive oil
½ cup chopped onion
¼ cup chopped red pepper
1 cup uncooked long grain white rice
2 cups chicken broth
Salt and pepper
1 bay leaf
¼ cup fresh peas

In skillet heat olive oil. Add onion and red pepper and cook until onion is transparent. Add rice and cook stirring, 2 to 3 minutes. Add broth, salt, and pepper, then add to taste bay leaf and parsley. Cover and bring to a boil.

Reduce heat and simmer gently for 20 minutes or until rice absorbs liquid. Discard bay.

Stir in peas, cover and let stand for 10 minutes before serving.

Roasted Pepper Salad
Serves 4

2 large green bell peppers
2 large yellow bell peppers
2 large red bell peppers
2 Tbsp. red wine vinegar
Dash salt
Freshly ground pepper
6 Tbsp. Spanish olive oil

Char peppers over gas flame or in broiler, turning occasionally, until skin blackens. Place in plastic bag; let stand for 10 minutes to steam. Peel and seed peppers, then cut into one-half inch wide strips and place in bowl. Mix together vinegar, salt, and pepper. Whisk in oil in a slow steady stream. Stir into peppers. Allow to stand at least 2 hours, and up to 24 hours, stirring occasionally. Serve at room temperature.

Roasted Russets with Garlic
Serves 6 to 8

3 lbs. small russets, halved
3 Tbsp. Spanish olive oil
½ tsp. salt
⅛ tsp. dry hot red pepper flakes
4 cloves garlic, thinly sliced
½ cup minced Italian parsley

In large roasting pan toss together potatotes, olive oil, salt, pepper flakes, and garlic. Roast in 350°F oven, tossing occasionally, for 1 hour. Add parsley; toss and serve.

Saffron Rice
Serves 4

2 Tbsp. Spanish olive oil
¼ cup finely chopped onion
1½ cups uncooked long grain white rice
3 cups boiling water
½ tsp. salt
¼ tsp. pulverized saffron threads

Heat oil in heavy twelve inch skillet until light haze forms. Add onions and cook until soft and transparent. Add rice and stir to coat with oil. Add water, salt, and saffron. Bring to a boil, stirring, then cover skillet tightly and reduce heat to lowest point. Simmer 20 minutes or until liquid has been absorbed.

Vegetables a la Vasca
Serves 6

½ cup Spanish olive oil
1/3 cup fresh lemon juice
5 cloves garlic
1 shallot, finely chopped
1 Tbsp. coriander seeds
½ tsp. salt
½ tsp. peppercorns
¼ lb. small onions, peeled
2 large carrots, peeled and cut into 1½" lengths
1 cup cauliflower flowerets
¼ lb. yellow summer squash, cut into ½" slices
¼ lb. zucchini, cut into ½" slices
1 vine-ripened tomato, chopped

Combine 2 cups water with oil, lemon juice, garlic, shallot, coriander seeds, salt, and peppercorns. Simmer, covered, for 10 minutes. Add onions and simmer, uncovered, 5 minutes. Add corrots and cauliflower and simmer 6 to 7 minutes longer. Add squash and cook for 5 additional minutes.

Transfer vegetables to shallow bowl. Cook liquid until it is reduced to 1 cup. Strain liquid, discarding solids, and pour over vegetables. Chill overnight. Sprinkle with chopped tomato just before serving.

Soups and Stews

When a fox starts preaching look to your hens.

Basque Proverb

Basque Garlic Soup
Serves 4

1 loaf French bread,
   sliced and allowed to dry out
¼ cup Spanish olive oil
6 garlic cloves, peeled
4 eggs, beaten
1½ tsp. sweet Spanish paprika
Water
¼ tsp. salt

Heat olive oil in Dutch oven. Lightly brown garlic cloves. Add sliced bread, paprika, salt, and enough water to cover bread. Simmer for 30 minutes. Whisk beaten eggs into simmering soup. Serve at once.

Basque Gazpacho
Serves 4

3 cups chopped vine-ripened tomatoes
1½ cups coarsely chopped sweet red pepper
1 cup coarsely chopped green pepper
2 cloves garlic, sliced
½ cup water
¼ cup Spanish olive oil
1/3 cup red wine vinegar
2 slices fresh bread, cubed

Combine all ingredients in food processor container and puree. Place kitchen sieve in large bowl. Pour mixture from food processor into sieve. Press solids with wooden spoon to extract as much liquid as possible. Discard solids. Season liquid with salt and pepper. Chill well before serving.

Bean Soup with Chorizos
Serves 6 to 7

4½ quarts water
1 lb. dried fava beans
2 large coarsely chopped onions
1½ Tbsp. finely chopped garlic
¼ lb. lean salt pork, rind removed
½ lb. chunk of prosciutto
3 chorizo
3 blood sausage
3 saffron threads, crushed
6 green peppercorns, crushed

In Dutch oven, bring 2 quarts water to boiling. Drop in beans and boil 2 minutes. Remove from heat and let beans soak for 1 hour. Drain beans, reserving liquid, and return to Dutch oven. Add enough fresh water to soaking liquid to make 4 quarts. Pour over beans. Add onions, garlic, and salt pork. Simmer 1 hour. Skim. Add ham and simmer 1 hour longer, or until beans are barely tender.

Simmer chorizos in one inch water in heavy skillet for 5 minutes. Drop chorizos and blood sausage into soup. Stir in saffron and cook for 30 minutes longer. Season with salt and pepper. Remove salt pork, ham and sausages. Cube ham and pork; slice sausages into one-half inch thick rounds. Return to soup and heat 3 to 5 minutes.

Good served with Dutch Oven Cornbread.

Chorizo and Kale Soup
Serves 5

½ lb. fresh kale, finely shredded
4 oz. chorizo, sliced into ¼" rounds
1 lb. medium russet potatoes,
    peeled and cut into ¼" rounds
5½ cups water
1 tsp. salt
½ cup Spanish olive oil
½ tsp. freshly ground pepper
¼ cup finely chopped Italian parsley

Simmer chorizo slices in water to cover for 15 minutes. Drain and set aside.

Combine potatoes, water and salt and cook until potatoes are tender. Transfer potatoes to bowl with slotted spoon and mash into smooth puree. Return mashed potatoes to cooking liquid along with olive oil, pepper, and greens. Simmer 5 minutes. Add chorizo and heat through. Serve at once.

Chick-Pea and Fresh Mint Soup

1 cup dried chick-peas (garbanzo beans)
1 Tbsp. Spanish olive oil
1 cup chopped onion
4 cloves garlic, minced
2 cups chicken stock
2 lbs. fresh tomatoes, peeled and chopped
¼ cup fresh mint leaves, chopped
Zest of ½ orange
½ tsp. sugar
½ cup minced Italian parsley
¼ tsp. freshly ground pepper

Soak chick-peas overnight. Heat oil in heavy skillet until light haze forms. Add ½ cup onion and the garlic. Cook 2 minutes. Drain chick-peas and add to skillet. Add stock and simmer for 3 minutes. Add tomatoes and cook 30 minutes longer. Add the mint, orange zest, sugar, and remaining onion; cover and simmer for 2 hours. Discard orange zest.

Just before serving, add parsley and pepper.

Cocido
(bean stew)
Serves 6 to 8

1 lb. dry pinto beans
Water
½ lb. salt pork, diced
1 cup chopped onion

Wash beans and sort. Soak in water to cover. Add more water, if necessary, to cover. Cook slowly until beans are tender.

In skillet, brown salt pork. Add onion and cook until soft and transparent. Stir contents of skillet into beans and heat 20 minutes longer.

Kale and Red Kidney Bean Soup
Serves 8

1 cup dried red kidney beans
6 cups water
1 lb. meaty lamb bones
8 oz. chorizo
½ cup dry split peas
1½ tsp. salt
6 cups torn kale
2 medium potatoes, peeled and diced
2 cups chopped cabbage

Soak kidney beans in water overnight. Drain and rinse.

In Dutch oven add beans and 6 cups water. Set aside. Brown lamb bones and chorizo. Add to beans along with split peas and salt. Simmer, covered, 2½ hours. Remove lamb bones. When cool enough to handle, remove meat from bones; cube. Return cubed lamb meat to Dutch oven.

Add remaining ingredients and simmer, covered, for 30 minutes.

Porrusalda
Serves 4

1 lb. salt cod
1 cup water
4 leeks
3 sweet red peppers, peeled and seeded
3 red potatoes, diced
1/3 cup Spanish olive oil
2 cloves garlic, minced
1 cup dry white wine
¼ cup minced fresh Italian parsley

Soak cod overnight, changing water at least 5 times. Cut fish into pieces. Place cod in Dutch oven with 1 cup water.

In heavy skillet heat olive oil until a light haze forms. Add potatoes and brown. Reduce heat and add leeks, red pepper and garlic. Cook until leeks are soft and transparent.

Add contents of skillet to Dutch oven. Add wine and parsley. Cover and cook until potatoes are tender.

Soupa a la Vizcaya
Serves 6

1 cup dried broad beans
6 cups water
1 lb. lean beef, cubed
½ lb. lean ham, cubed
¼ lb. salt pork, diced
1 onion
4 cloves garlic
4 ripe tomatoes, chopped
3 lbs. cut-up fryer chicken
1 lb. potatoes, cubed
1 medium cabbage, chopped
Salt and pepper to taste

Soak beans overnight in water to cover. Drain and rinse. Put in large pot with 6 cups water. Add beef, ham, salt pork, onion, garlic, and tomatoes. Simmer gently 1 hour. Add chicken and cook 45 minutes. Add potatoes and cabbage; cook until potatoes are tender. Season with salt and pepper.

White Bean and Sausage Soup
Serves 4

1 cup dried Great Northern beans
2½ quarts water
½ lb. lean ham, cubed
2 oz. piece salt pork
1 medium onion, finely chopped
1/3 lb. chorizo
½ lb. turnip greens, shredded
2 medium potatoes, peeled and diced

In Dutch oven bring water to boil. Add beans and boil briskly for 2 minutes. Remove from heat and let beans soak for 1 hour. Add ham, salt pork, and onion. Simmer, partially covered, 1½ hours. Add chorizo, greens, and potatoes; simmer for 30 minutes. Remove sausage and salt pork. Discard pork. Slice chorizo into ¼" thick rounds. Return to soup and serve.

Wine Braised Lamb and Pork Stew
Serves 5

1 lb. boneless pork shoulder, cut into 2" cubes
1 lb. boneless lamb shoulder, cut into 2" pieces
1 cup dry white wine
¼ cup minced Italian parsley
1 bay leaf
½ tsp. dried thyme, crumbled
¼ tsp. salt
¼ tsp. freshly ground pepper
4 large onions, thinly sliced
4 large baking potatoes,
    scrubbed and cut into ½" thick slices
1/3 cup Spanish olive oil

Combine meats, wine, parsley, herbs, and seasonings in large bowl. Marinate in refrigerator overnight.

Next day, heat oil in heavy skillet until light haze forms. Add potatoes and cook until lightly browned.

Preheat oven to 350°F. Butter 5 quart casserole. Cover bottom of casserole with ¼ of the onions and ¼ of the fried potatoes. Top with 1/3 of the meat mixture. Continue with three more vegetable layers and 2 more meat layers. Pour in marinade. Cover casserole and bake 1½ hours.

Fish and Seafood

*Fish and guests go bad after three days
and must be tossed out.*

Basque Proverb

Alavian Seafood Stew
Serves 4 to 5

1 tsp. saffron threads
½ cup boiling water
¼ cup Spanish olive oil
1 cup coarsely chopped green pepper
4 cloves garlic, chopped
2 ripe tomatoes, chopped
1/3 cup dry white wine
1 bay leaf
2 Tbsp. chopped Italian parsley
1 Tbsp. chopped fresh thyme
Salt and pepper
1 lb. squid, cleaned and cut into 1″ pieces
1 lb. shrimp, shelled and deveined
1 dozen small clams, well rinsed
1 dozen mussels, scrubbed

Place saffron in cup and add boiling water. Let stand 2 hours.

Heat oil in Dutch oven and add green pepper and garlic. Cook until garlic begins to turn a very light brown. Add tomatoes, water with saffron, wine, bay, parsley, thyme, salt, and pepper to taste. Simmer 10 minutes, uncovered.

Add squid, shrimp, clams, and mussels. Simmer 5 minutes. Serve at once.

Good with rice.

Bacaloa al pil-pil
(Basque salt cod)
Serves 5

1½ lbs. salt cod
1 egg, slightly beaten
Flour
3 sweet red peppers,
    roasted, seeded, and peeled
Spanish olive oil
2 cloves garlic, minced

Soak cod overnight, changing water at least five to six times. Cut fish into 5 pieces. Cut roasted peppers into strips.

Add olive oil to heavy skillet to one-quarter inch depth and heat over high flame until light haze forms. Meanwhile dip cod pieces in egg and then lightly dredge in flour.

Reduce heat to medium low and add cod pieces, peppers, and garlic. Cook until cod is a golden brown.

Put cod in shallow pan, top with peppers and bake at 300°F for 1 hour.

Cod with Clams in Parsley Sauce
Serves 6

½ cup Spanish olive oil
4 cloves garlic, minced
2½ cups minced fresh Italian parsley
3 Tbsp. flour
3 lbs. cod fillets, cut into 6 portions
36 clams
1½ cups white fish stock (recipe follows)
½ cup dry white wine

Heat oil in heavy skillet until light haze forms. Add garlic, 1 cup parsley, and flour. Cook, stirring, for 2 minutes. Add cod, stock and wine. Bring liquid to simmering and cook, covered, 3 minutes. Transfer fish to warm plate and keep warm. Add remaining parsley and clams to stock. Simmer, covered, 3 to 5 minutes or until clams pop open. Season with salt and pepper, if desired.

Divide cod among 6 heated soup plates. Add clams and sauce. Serve at once.

White Fish Stock

1 lb. bones and trimmings from any white fish
1 cup chopped onion
¼ cup chopped Italian parsley
2 Tbsp. fresh lime juice
½ tsp. salt
½ cup dry sherry

In well-buttered heavy saucepan, combine bones and trimmings, onion, parsley, and lime juice. Steam, covered, over high heat for 5 minutes. Add 3½ cups cold water and sherry. Bring to boil, skimming the froth, and cook for 25 minutes. Strain through several layers of cheese cloth, pressing solids to extract all liquid. Makes 3 cups.

Crab Meat Gazpacho
Serves 6

½ medium onion, chopped
½ cucumber, chopped
2 medium vine-ripened tomatoes,
    peeled and chopped
½ green pepper, chopped
½ red pepper, chopped
2 Tbsp. Spanish olive oil
Juice of 1 lemon
5 cups tomato juice
⅛ tsp. red pepper flakes
1 clove garlic, minced
1 Tbsp. honey
½ lb. crab meat
1 medium-sized ripe avocado,
    peeled and chopped
1/3 cup chopped Italian parsley

In food processor combine onion, cucumber, tomato, red and green peppers, and olive oil. Blend well until all vegetables are finely chopped.

Pour into large bowl and stir in tomato juice, lemon juice, red pepper flakes, garlic, and honey.

Add 3 cups ice cubes and stir gazpacho until ice is melted.

Divide crab among 6 bowls. Add avocado and parsley to each. Ladle gazpacho into bowls. Serve at once.

Fried Salt Cod
Serves 4

1 lb. dried salt cod, cut into 3×5″ pieces
1/3 cup Spanish olive oil
4 cloves garlic, crushed
¼ cup diced salt pork
Flour
¼ tsp. freshly ground pepper
3 Tbsp. freshly squeezed lemon juice

Soak cod in water to cover and store in cool place for 24 hours, changing water 5 to 6 times. Drain fish; rinse well and pat dry. Heat oil in heavy skillet over medium-low heat. Add garlic and salt pork and cook until fat is rendered. Discard garlic and unmelted fat. Increase heat to medium-high. Combine flour and pepper on plate. Dip fish in flour mixture to coat lightly. Add fish to skillet and cook until golden and just beginning to flake, turning once. Transfer fish to heated platter. Stir lemon juice into ¼ cup pan drippings and pour over fish. Garnish with lemon wedges, if desired.

Marinated Trout with Herbs
Serves 4

¾ cup dry red wine
¼ cup Spanish olive oil
2/3 cup finely chopped onion
1½ Tbsp. finely cut fresh mint
½ tsp. dried rosemary
½ tsp. dried thyme
20 whole black peppercorns
½ tsp. salt
4 trout (8 to 12 oz. each)
3 egg yolks, lightly beaten

Lay fish in one layer in oven-proof dish.

Combine red wine, oil, onion, mint, herbs, peppercorns, and salt. Pour over fish and let stand for 30 minutes. Turn and marinate 15 minutes longer.

Bake in preheated 350°F oven for 25 minutes or until fish is firm to the touch. Transfer fish to heated platter and keep warm.

Strain cooking liquid through several layers of cheese cloth, squeezing out as much liquid as possible. Whisk ¼ cup liquid into beaten egg yolks, then whisk mixture into remaining liquid in pan. Heat slowly, whisking constantly, until the sauce thickens slightly. Do not allow to boil.

Pour sauce over fish and serve at once.

Pickled Whitefish Fillets

1 cup Spanish olive oil
3 lbs. whitefish fillets
3 large onions, sliced and separated into rings
2 sweet red peppers, cut into rings
1 sweet green pepper, cut into rings
4 medium carrots, grated
1 cup white wine vinegar
1 bay leaf
4 cloves garlic, minced
Juice of 2 limes
½ cup minced Italian parsley

Heat ½ cup olive oil in skillet. Fry fillets 3 to 5 minutes on each side. Drain on paper towels. In clean skillet heat remaining oil. Add onions and cook 3 minutes, then add pepper and cook 2 minutes. Add carrots, vinegar, bay, and garlic. Cook 5 minutes. Stir in lime juice and parsley.

Place fish in glass dish. Pour skillet ingredients over fish, cover and chill at least 2 days. Serve as an appetizer. Fish will keep 1 week refrigerated.

Poached Salmon Fillets with Tomato and Almond Sauce
Serves 4

¼ cup Spanish olive oil
½ cup minced onions
1½ Tbsp. minced garlic
¼ cup almond paste
¼ cup crumbled white bread
4 tomatoes, peeled, seeded, and chopped
Juice of 1 lemon
4 salmon steaks
¼ cup sliced almonds, toasted
2 Tbsp. chopped Italian parsley

Heat oil in heavy ten inch skillet over medium heat until light haze forms. Add onions and garlic; cook until onions are soft and transparent. Add almond paste and bread. Stir to blend. Add tomatoes, increase heat and simmer until most of the liquid evaporates.

In a twelve inch skillet, bring 6 cups water to boil. Add juice of lemon and salt. Reduce heat. Add salmon steaks and simmer, uncovered, 5 to 8 minutes or until fish flakes easily. Transfer fish to heated platter. Reheat sauce and add enough fish stock to make sauce the consistency of a light gravy. Pour sauce over fish and serve garnished with sliced toasted almonds and parsley.

Salmon in Sherry Sauce
Serves 4 to 6

2 lbs. salmon steaks, cut ¾" thick
2 Tbsp. Spanish olive oil
Coarse salt
8 peppercorns, crushed
2 16-oz. cans tomato sauce
2 cloves garlic, pressed
12 pitted green olives, drained and rinsed
1 cup dry sherry

Rub salmon with olive oil. Sprinkle salt and crushed peppercorns over fish.

In skillet, cook tomato sauce, garlic and olives, uncovered, over medium heat for 15 to 20 minutes, stirring occasionally. Stir in sherry. Lay salmon in skillet, spooning sauce over. Cover skillet and cook over low heat for 10 to 15 mintues or until fish is firm.

Salt Cod with Potatoes and Onions
Serves 4

1 lb. dried salt cod
1 cup olive oil
6 medium russet potatoes,
    peeled and sliced into ½" thick slices
4 medium onions,
    sliced and separated into rings
1 tsp. minced garlic
20 pitted black olives
4 hard-cooked eggs, sliced
¼ cup chopped Italian parsley

Soak cod overnight in at least 5 changes of water.

Cook potatoes until just tender. Drain cod and rinse. Place cod in saucepan and add enough fresh water to cover by one inch. Simmer 20 minutes. Drain and set aside.

Heat ½ cup oil in twelve inch skillet until light haze forms. Add onion rings and cook until soft and transparent. Stir in garlic and remove skillet from heat.

Spread ½ of the potatoes in bottom of buttered eight inch casserole. Add half the cod, then half the onions. Repeat layers. Pour remaining oil over top.

Bake in 250°F oven for 35 to 40 minutes. Garnish with egg slices, olives and parsley.

Snapper with Wine and Saffron Sauce
Serves 4

2 Tbsp. Spanish olive oil
4 shallots, minced
½ cup dry white wine
½ cup clam juice
1 lb. red snapper fillets
1 cup cream
3 red peppers,
    roasted, peeled, seeded, and chopped
½ cup dry white wine
Juice of 1 lime
½ cup cream
1 tsp. minced garlic
1 tsp. saffron threads, crumbled

Sprinkle bottom of glass or ceramic baking pan with olive oil, shallots, wine and clam juice. Lay snapper in pan, cover and cook in preheated 375°F oven for 10 to 12 minutes.

Transfer fish to platter and keep warm. Reduce liquid in baking pan over high heat by half. Add cream and cook until it is reduced by half.

Puree peppers in food processor. Combine wine, lime juice, ½ cup cream, garlic and saffron in saucepan and cook until reduced by half. Add to snapper cooking liquid along with pureed pepper and cook together until thick enough to coat a spoon. Season with salt and pepper and serve over fish.

Squid in Ink Sauce
Serves 4

2 lbs. small squid with ink sacs
½ cup Spanish olive oil
2 onions, finely chopped
3 cloves garlic, minced
¼ cup finely chopped Italian parsley
1 cup fish broth
2 Tbsp. all purpose flour
½ cup tomato puree (preferably fresh)
⅛ tsp. freshly grated nutmeg

To clean squid, grasp tail and head firmly and pull the fin and outer portion of tail away from head and tentacles. Carefully remove small grey ink sac from the inner section of the tail and set aside in small bowl. With a sharp knife cut tentacles free, just below the eyes. Discard intestines and eye section. Remove cartilage from the tentacle base and discard. Remove tail skeleton from inside tail section and discard. Pull fins away from tail; set aside. Under cold running water, rub membrane from fins and tail section. Rinse parts well.

Slice tails into ½" wide rings. Cut tentacle sections into 3 pieces and slice each fin in half.

In heavy skillet heat olive oil over high heat until light haze forms. Add squid, onions, garlic, and parsley; cook, uncovered, 5 to 6 minutes, stirring. Reduce heat. Cover and simmer 20 minutes.

Meanwhile mash ink sac in sieve to remove as much ink as possible. Pour broth over sacs and mash again. With whisk, beat flour into broth/ink mixture until smooth. Add tomato puree and nutmeg. Pour over simmering squid, stirring constantly. Increase heat and bring mixture to a boil. Immediately reduce heat to low and simmer 5 minutes, covered. Turn off heat and allow to stand 5 minutes before serving.

Good with hot rice.

Steelhead with Onions and Peppers
Serves 6

2 lb. steelhead steaks
6 medium onions, sliced and separated into rings
2 red sweet peppers, roasted, seeded, peeled,
    and cut into strips
3 green peppers, roasted, seeded, peeled, and
    cut into strips
2 cloves garlic, crushed
¼ cup Spanish olive oil
4 large vine-ripened tomatoes, peeled and
    chopped
2 yellow chiles, diced
Salt and freshly ground pepper

Heat oil in heavy skillet until light haze forms. Add onions, red and green peppers. Cook until onions are soft and transparent. Add garlic and remove from heat.

Arrange steaks in baking pan. Add sauteed vegetables, tomatoes, yellow chiles, salt, and pepper. Cover and bake at 350°F for 30 to 40 minutes or until fish flakes easily.

Tvirlak
Clams in parsley sauce
Serves 6

4 lbs. clams
½ cup cornmeal
½ cup Spanish olive oil
½ cup minced onion
3 cloves garlic, minced
1½ cups finely chopped Italian parsley
¾ cup white wine
¼ cup freshly squeezed lemon juice
2 cups cracker crumbs

Place clams in large pan of cool water. Sprinkle ½ cup cornmeal over water and allow clams to stand 4 to 5 hours or over night. (Clams will take in the cornmeal and eject the sand.) Drain and rinse clams well.

Heat oil in large Dutch oven. Add onion and garlic and saute 3 to 5 minutes. Add parsley and clams, cover and steam until clams open. Add wine and lemon juice. Stir in cracker crumbs. Divide clams among 6 individual bowls and spoon sauce over top. Serve at once.

Meat

*A charitable man gives a poor man the trotters
of a stolen lamb.*

Basque Proverb

Basque Dutch Oven Dinner
Serves 10

½ cup chicken fat
3 lbs. onions, halved and thinly sliced
3 cloves garlic, sliced
2 green peppers, seeded and cubed
5 lbs. lean beef, cut into 1 inch cubes
1 lb. ripe tomatoes, chopped
1 Tbsp. chopped cilantro
1 tsp. crumbled saffron threads
2 cups tomato puree
Hot rice

In Dutch oven melt chicken fat; add onions and garlic and cook until onions are wilted. Add green pepper, beef, tomatoes, cilantro, and saffron. Salt and pepper to taste. Carefully stir in puree. Bring to boiling on stove top, then cover and cook in preheated 325°F oven for 2½ to 3 hours.

Serve hot directly from Dutch oven. Spoon over hot rice.

Blood Sausages

12 lbs. yellow onions, finely chopped
18 leeks, white portion only, finely chopped
4½ lbs. lard, unprocessed
2½ quarts uncoagulated blood
3 hot red peppers, minced
1 Tbsp. ground cloves
1 Tbsp. ground anise seed
3 Tbsp. black pepper
2 Tbsp. powdered oregano
1 Tbsp. ground cinnamon
3 Tbsp. salt

On very low heat, cook leeks and onions in 1 lb. lard for 8 hours. Grind remaining 3½ lbs. lard and mix with blood. Then mix in warm onions and leeks.

Add remaining ingredients, mixing to blend well. Stuff into sausage casings according to casing instructions, and tie off into links. Scald sausages in briskly boiling water until mixture is well coagulated. Cool and freeze that which is not for immediate use.

To cook, simmer sausages in broth 30 minutes, or bake in 375°F oven for 30 to 35 minutes. Some prefer their sausages fried in hot fat.

Boiled Lambs' Tongues

6 or 7 lambs' tongues
2½ quarts water
1 Tbsp. salt
2 tsp. peppercorns, crushed
1 large onion, sliced
½ cup chopped celery tops
¼ cup minced Italian parsley
2 slices lemon

Clean tongues and simmer in 2½ quarts water to which remaining ingredients have been added. Cook 55 minutes. Remove tongues from liquid. When cool enough to handle, peel and core.

Split and serve hot with tomato sauce or chilled with horseradish or mustard dressing.

Braised Lamb with Cilantro and Lemon
Serves 4 to 5

2 lbs. 1 inch lamb cubes
1 Tbsp. lard
¾ cup dry white wine
1½ tsp. ground cumin seed
2 Tbsp. chopped cilantro
1 tsp. finely chopped garlic
½ tsp. salt
Freshly ground pepper
6 thin slices lemon, halved

In heavy 12 inch skillet, melt lard over high heat. Add lamb cubes and brown them evenly. Stir in ½ cup wine, cumin, garlic, salt, and pepper. Simmer, covered, for 30 minutes. Add remaining wine and lemon slices and cook over high heat, stirring carefully once or twice, until sauce thickens. Stir in cilantro.

Good served with Basque potatoes.

Callos al Ferial
(tripe with chorizo and ham)

2 lbs. honeycomb tripe
2 medium onions, thinly sliced
1/3 cup Spanish olive oil
2 chorizo, thinly sliced
¼ lb. lean ham, cubed
¼ tsp. black pepper
¼ tsp. cayenne

Cover tripe with water. Add 1 Tbsp. salt and simmer, covered, 1½ hours.

Meanwhile, heat olive oil in heavy skillet over high heat until light haze forms. Reduce heat to low and add onion, chorizo, and ham. Stir a few minutes until onion wilts; reduce heat and cook slowly for 30 minutes. Add pepper and cayenne.

Drain tripe and pat dry. Cut into serving pieces. Add tripe to chorizo mixture and heat through. Serve at once.

Casserole of Lamb, Lemon, and Wine
Serves 4

4 lbs. shoulder steaks with bone
Coarse salt
10 peppercorns, crushed
4 medium onions, sliced
2 small lemons, thinly sliced
4 cloves garlic, crushed
¼ cup fresh cilantro leaves
1½ cups dry white wine
1 cup water
¼ cup Spanish olive oil

Rub meat with mixture of salt and pepper. Layer onions, lamb, and lemon in large casserole. Sprinkle with garlic and cilantro. Add wine, water, and olive oil. Bake, covered, at 300°F for 2 hours.

Dutch Oven Dinner
Serves 8

1 cup dried chickpeas
5½ quarts water
6 lbs. stewing hen (or wild sage hens)
2 lbs. fresh beef brisket
1 lb. lean smoked ham
½ lb. salt pork
2 large onions, peeled
2 Tbsp. minced garlic
¼ cup chopped Italian parsley
2 carrots, unpeeled
6 chorizos
1 cabbage, cut into 6 wedges
4 large russet potatoes,
    unpeeled, cut into lengths
Salt and pepper to taste

Soak chickpeas in water to cover overnight. Drain and rinse. Place in Dutch oven; add 5½ quarts water, fowl, and brisket. Simmer, covered, 2 hours. Skim foam occasionally. Add ham, salt pork, onions, garlic, parsley, and carrots. Cook 30 minutes.

Simmer chorizos in water to cover for 5 minutes. Add to Dutch oven along with cabbage and potatoes. Cook 30 minutes.

Serve cooking broth as first course. Carve meats and poultry and arrange on platter with vegetables. Serve.

Lamb Chops with Tomatoes and Olives
Serves 6

6 lamb chops
Flour
Salt and pepper
2 Tbsp. Spanish olive oil
1/3 cup dry white wine
1 lb. vine-ripened tomatoes, peeled,
   seeded, and chopped
½ cup Spanish olives, seeded and sliced

Season chops with salt and pepper; dredge with flour. Heat oil in heavy skillet until light haze forms. Add chops and cook 5 to 6 minutes on each side. Transfer to heated platter.

Pour wine into skillet and scrape up brown bits. Stir in tomatoes and olives. Cook over medium heat for 4 to 5 minutes. Season with salt and pepper. Spoon over chops.

Lamb and Chorizo Casserole
Serves 4 to 5

2 cups dry navy beans
6 cups water
1½ lbs. 1 inch lamb cubes
1 cup seeded and chopped green pepper
½ cup chopped onion
3 cloves garlic, minced
1 lb. chorizo
3 Tbsp. Spanish olive oil
4 ripe tomatoes, chopped
¼ cup chopped Italian parsley
¼ tsp. salt

Soak beans overnight in water to cover. Drain and rinse.

In Dutch oven mix beans with 6 cups water, lamb, green pepper, onion, and garlic. Simmer, covered, 1½ hours.

Brown chorizo in olive oil.

Drain bean mixture, reserving liquid. Return bean mixture to Dutch oven. Add remaining ingredients and 1 cup reserved liquid. Cover and bake at 325°F 1 to 1½ hours, adding more liquid if necessary.

Lamb Fries

Clean and remove outer skin or sac of testicles of young male lambs. Rinse and drain well. Cut into slices. Heat olive oil in heavy skillet; add a couple of cloves of minced garlic. Add sliced lamb fries and brown lightly over medium heat. Season with salt and freshly ground pepper.

Lamb's Liver with Red Wine Sauce
Serves 4 to 5

1 cup dry red wine
1 Tbsp. red wine vinegar
2 tsp. minced fresh garlic
1 bay leaf
¼ tsp. salt
1 lb. lamb's liver, cut into ¼ inch slices
3 Tbsp. Spanish olive oil
3 slices bacon, chopped
3 Tbsp. finely chopped Italian parsley

Combine wine, vinegar, garlic, bay, and salt in glass baking dish. Add liver and coat well with marinade. Marinate at room temperature for three to four hours.

Heat olive oil in heavy 12 inch skillet until light haze forms. Add bacon and cook until browned and crisp. Drain on paper towels. Remove liver from marinade and pat dry. Brown liver in pan drippings for 2 minutes on each side. Remove to heated platter.

Pour marinade into hot skillet and boil, uncovered, until reduced by half.

Scatter bacon pieces over liver, pour marinade on top and sprinkle with parsley. Serve at once.

Good with Basque Potatoes.

Leg of Lamb with Lemon-Garlic Sauce
Serves 5 to 6

3 lb. leg of lamb
½ cup Spanish olive oil
½ cup freshly squeezed lemon juice
4 to 6 cloves garlic, minced
Freshly ground pepper
Salt

Place lamb in shallow glass dish. Slowly whisk oil into lemon juice. Pour over meat. Sprinkle with garlic and generous amount of pepper. Chill 24 hours, turning occasionally.

Bring lamb to room temperature. Preheat oven to 325°F. Place leg and marinade in shallow roasting pan. Sprinkle with salt. Roast 2 to 3 hours, depending on desired doneness, basting frequently with pan juices.

Slice and serve with pan juices.

Pork and Green Pepper Pie
Serves 8

1 lb. lean pork roast
    cut into ⅛ inch by 3 inch strips
½ tsp. dried oregano
¼ tsp. crumbled saffron threads
¼ cup minced Italian parsley
2 cloves garlic, minced
½ cup Spanish olive oil
2 onions, sliced
3 green bell peppers, peeled, seeded, and cut
    into ½ inch wide strips
¼ cup dry white wine
Pastry for 9 inch, 2 crust pie

In bowl, toss pork with oregano, saffron, parsley, garlic, and ¼ cup olive oil. Cover bowl and let pork marinade overnight, turning occasionally.

Heat ¼ cup olive oil in Dutch oven or heavy skillet until light haze forms. Add onions and green pepper and saute a couple of minutes. Reduce heat to moderate, cover and cook 15 minutes. Remove vegetables from skillet. Add pork and marinade, and cook over high heat, stirring, 1 minute. Add wine and cook 1 to 2 minutes longer. Remove from heat, add onions and peppers. Season to taste with salt and pepper. When cool, spoon into uncooked pie shell, adjust top crust and crimp edges. Bake in preheated 400°F oven for 10 minutes. Reduce heat to 350°F and bake 45 to 50 minutes longer. Cut into wedges when partially cool and serve warm.

Rice with Ham and Shrimp
Serves 6

½ cup Spanish olive oil
¼ lb. chorizo, thinly sliced
2 medium onions, finely chopped
4 cloves garlic, minced
3 cups chicken broth
3 medium tomatoes, finely chopped
2 medium green peppers,
   seeded and cut into strips
3 Tbsp. chopped Italian parsley
2 tsp. sugar
½ tsp. salt
1 tsp. ground cumin
½ tsp. freshly ground pepper
2 cups uncooked short grained white rice
1 lb. medium shrimp, cleaned
½ lb. lean ham, cut into 1½ inch cubes

Heat oil in Dutch oven until light haze forms. Add chorizo, onion, and garlic and cook until chorizo is browned and onions are soft (approximately 5 minutes). Stir in remaining ingredients except rice, shrimp, and ham. Cook 10 minutes. Add rice and cook, covered, over medium heat until almost tender (approximately 12 minutes). Stir in shrimp and ham. Cook for 8 to 10 minutes, or until all liquid has been absorbed. Serve as an entree with a hearty loaf of bread.

Roast Leg of Pork
Serves 12 to 14

1 12 lb. leg of fresh pork, skin removed
4 cloves of garlic, crushed
1 tsp. salt
12 peppercorns, crushed
8 allspice berries, crushed
8 juniper berries, crushed
1 Tbsp. fresh thyme leaves
1 bay leaf, crushed
2 3 inch strips orange zest
1 large onion, quartered
Red wine
Olive oil

Combine garlic, salt, peppercorns, allspice, juniper, thyme, and bay. Rub leg with mixture and place in deep roasting pan. Add onion and zest. Cover roast with warm red wine. Let marinade 5 to 6 days refrigerated, turning two or three times a day.

Remove roast from marinade and dry well. Rub with olive oil. Place roast in a clean roasting pan. Roast at 300°F allowing 25 minutes per pound. Baste every 30 minutes with heated marinade. Transfer to a hot platter, strain juices in pan, and remove excess fat. Strain any remaining marinade and add to pan juices. Cook juices down to two cups. Serve with roast.

Spring Lamb Stew
Serves 4 to 5

2 lbs. lamb, cut into 1 inch cubes
1/3 cup flour
1 cup chopped onion
3 Tbsp. Spanish olive oil
1½ cups hot water
1 bay leaf
2 tsp. salt
½ tsp. whole peppercorns
1 sweet red pepper, diced
1 green pepper, diced
1 cup chopped ripe tomato
1½ cups fresh garden peas
Juice of 1 lemon

Dredge lamb in flour. In Dutch oven, cook onion in olive oil until golden. Add lamb and brown. Add water, salt, peppercorns and bay; cover and cook slowly for 1½ hours. Add peppers, tomatoes and peas. Simmer, uncovered, 15 minutes. Season with lemon juice.

Tongue with Wild Mushroom Sauce
Serves 4

1 beef tongue
2 Tbsp. salt
3 cloves of garlic
Salt and pepper
¼ lb. chopped Boletus edulus, or other
   fresh mild flavored wild mushroom
1 medium onion, chopped
2 cloves garlic, minced
Flour
1 egg
½ cup Spanish olive oil
2 Tbsp. tomato puree
2 cups cooking broth (from tongue)
2 cups red wine
¼ cup grated carrot
Bouquet garni made of rosemary, thyme,
   oregano, and Italian parsley

Simmer tongue in water to cover, seasoned with salt and garlic. Remove tongue from water when tender. Reserve 2 cups cooking liquid. When tongue is cool enough to handle, remove and discard the dark outer skin. Chill tongue 2 to 4 hours. Slice tongue and season with salt and pepper.

Dip tongue in flour, then beaten egg, and then again in flour. Cook slices in hot olive oil in skillet until lightly browned. Keep warm in ovenproof dish.

Make sauce by adding mushrooms, onion, and garlic to remaining oil in skillet. Cook until onions are golden. Add remaining ingredients and simmer for 15 minutes. Pour over tongue slices and bake at 300°F for 20 minutes.

Basque-Style Chorizo

1½ tsp. cumin seeds
1½ tsp. dried red pepper flakes
2 tsp. coriander seeds

1 tsp. granulated sugar
2½ tsp. coarse salt
1 Tbsp. paprika
½ tsp. whole black peppercorns
6 cloves garlic, minced
1½ lbs. lean pork, cut into 2 to 3 inch strips
½ lb. fresh pork fat, cut into 1 inch dice
½ cup hearty red wine
Natural sausage casings (available at
    butcher shops and some meat counters
    at large grocery stores)

Combine cumin seeds, pepper flakes, and coriander seeds in small skillet or pan and shake over moderate heat until the seeds begin to crackle. Combine toasted seeds with sugar, salt, paprika, and peppercorns, then toss with pork strips and pork fat.

Using a medium-coarse disc, grind the seasoned pork with meat grinder. When all meat has been ground, add wine and mix well.

Remove a length of sausage casing from brine and rinse well. Fit casing over faucet and allow water to flow through casing. Should holes appear cut out the damaged portion. Place rinsed casings in bowl of luke-warm water.

Cut lengths of cotton string into 3 inch pieces for tying links. Cut casings into 35 inch lengths. Tie one end of casing with cotton string, leaving one inch of casing at the tip. Using a funnel or pastry bag, pipe meat mixture into casing, working mixture gently to tied end. When casing has been filled to 2 inches of top of casing, remove from funnel or pastry bag and tie securely with cotton string. Tie links in casing at 8 inch intervals. Hang the string of sausage in an airy place for 3 to 4 hours. Wrap in freezer paper and freeze sausages if they are not to be eaten for two or three days, otherwise refrigerate.

To cook, prick chorizo all over with a pin. Place the string of sausages in a large skillet with ½ inch water and heat them over moderate heat, turning frequently, until the water evaporates and the sausages have browned.

Poultry

There is never trust without loss.

Basque Proverb

Basque Poultry Empanada
Serves 6 to 8

3 Tbsp. Spanish olive oil
1 small red pepper,
    peeled, seeded, and chopped
2 green bell peppers,
    peeled, seeded, and chopped
1 medium onion, diced
2 large ripe tomatoes, peeled and chopped
1 clove garlic, minced
½ cup lean ham, diced
2 cups diced cooked poultry
¼ tsp. salt
Dash red pepper flakes

Dough:
¼ tsp. sugar
1 cup warm milk
2 pkg. active dry yeast
4 cups all purpose flour
¼ cup butter, melted and cooled slightly
1 egg
1 egg yolk, beaten

To make filling, heat olive oil in skillet over high heat until light haze forms. Reduce heat to medium and cook peppers, onion and garlic until soft. Add tomatoes, ham, and poultry. Simmer 5 minutes. Season with salt and pepper flakes. Preheat oven to 400°F.

For dough, stir sugar into warm milk and sprinkle yeast over the liquid. Let stand 5 minutes. Stir.

Sift flour into large bowl. Lightly beat butter and 1 egg into yeast mixture. Beat yeast mixture into sifted flour. When dough is formed, knead on lightly floured surface until smooth and elastic.

Sprinkle dough lightly with flour, cover with damp cloth and let rise until double in bulk. Knead risen dough lightly. Divide dough in half. On lightly floured surface roll dough to two 12 inch rounds. Place one round on greased baking sheet and spread filling to ½ inch from edge. Place second round on top and press edges together to seal, using tines of fork. Brush with beaten egg. Let Empanada rest 1 hour, then bake in preheated oven for 45 minutes or until golden brown. Good served hot or cold.

Basque Style Paella
Serves 6 to 8

4 whole chicken breasts, halved
Salt and freshly ground pepper
¼ cup butter, melted
¼ tsp. ground coriander seed
1/3 cup cooking sherry
4 cloves garlic, minced
1 medium onion, chopped
1½ cups long grain white rice
1/3 cup Spanish olive oil
1 green pepper, cut in ½ inch long strips
2 cups clam broth
1 cup chicken broth
1 lb. ripe tomatoes, chopped
½ tsp. salt
1½ tsp. sugar
1 lb. medium-sized shrimp,
  shelled and deveined
1 dozen clams
Dash cayenne pepper
¾ cup pimento-stuffed green olives

Place chicken breasts, skin side up, in greased 13×9×2″ baking pan. Season with salt and pepper. Brush with melted butter. Sprinkle with coriander, cover with foil and bake at 350°F for 40 minutes. Uncover; sprinkle with sherry and bake 20 minutes longer, basting occasionally with pan drippings.

Cook garlic, onion, and rice in hot olive oil in large skillet until golden. Add green pepper, broth, tomatoes, salt and sugar. Cover and simmer gently for 25 minutes. Stir occasionally.

Stir in chicken, shrimp, clams, cayenne, and olives. Cover and continue cooking 5 minutes, or until clams pop open and liquid is absorbed.

Braised Chicken with Almond and Garlic Sauce
Serves 4 to 5

4 lbs. chicken, cut-up
Salt and pepper
1 cup flour
½ cup Spanish olive oil
2 cups finely chopped Italian parsley
1½ cups dry white wine
1½ cups water
2 Tbsp. almond paste
2 hard-cooked egg yolks
1½ Tbsp. minced garlic
¼ tsp. crumbled saffron threads

Sprinkle chicken with salt and pepper; dip pieces in flour and shake off excess.

Heat oil in heavy 12 inch skillet until a light haze forms, then brown chicken. Transfer browned chicken to 6 quart casserole.

Pour off all but 3 tablespoons drippings. Add onions and cook until soft and transparent. Spread over chicken. Pour wine and water over chicken and cover. Simmer 20 minutes.

In food processor (or with mortar and pestle) mix almond paste, egg yolks, garlic and saffron to a smooth paste. Thin with ¼ cup liquid from casserole, then gradually stir into chicken mixture. Cover and cook 10 minutes or until chicken is tender.

Transfer chicken to warm platter. Boil liquid until reduced by half. Pour over chicken. Serve at once. Great with hot steamed rice.

Chicken and Chorizo with Rice
Serves 5 to 6

½ cup diced salt pork
2 cups finely chopped onion
3 cloves garlic, minced
2 green peppers, seeded and chopped
1 red sweet pepper, seeded and chopped
1½ lb. chorizo
4 cups chicken broth
Salt and pepper
1 dozen pimento stuffed green olives
½ tsp. crushed saffron threads
3 lbs. cut-up fryer pieces
1 Tbsp. paprika
¼ cup Spanish olive oil
2 cups uncooked long grain white rice
1 cup fresh peas

In Dutch oven combine salt pork, onion, garlic, green pepper, red pepper, and chorizo. Cook together until onions are wilted. Add ¼ cup broth, salt, and pepper to taste, then olives and saffron. Set aside.

Sprinkle chicken with salt, pepper, and paprika. Brown in hot olive oil, then place in Dutch oven. Stir in rice, remaining broth and chorizo mixture; cover and bake in preheated 375°F oven for 1 hour. Uncover, stir in peas and bake 10 minutes longer.

Chicken and Rice, Basque Style
Serves 4

3 lbs. chicken, cut-up
1/3 cup olive oil
3 cloves garlic, minced
2 onions, chopped
2 green peppers, seeded and chopped
2 tomatoes, chopped
2 cups diced lean ham
Dash red pepper flakes

2 cups long grain white rice
4 cups chicken broth
1 tsp. saffron threads
½ cup frozen peas
1 red pepper, cut into strips
2 Tbsp. Italian parsley, chopped

In Dutch oven brown chicken in hot olive oil. Add garlic, onion, and green pepper and saute for 5 minutes. Add tomatoes, ham, red pepper flakes, rice, broth, and saffron. Place in 350°F preheated oven and bake for 35 minutes. Add peas and red pepper; cook 10 minutes. Sprinkle with parsley. Serve at once.

Chicken with Saffron Sauce
Serves 6 to 7

5 lbs. cut-up fryer pieces
¼ cup chopped Italian parsley
1 onion, quartered
2 quarts water
Salt and pepper
5 Tbsp. Spanish olive oil
1 cup finely chopped onion
2 shallots, finely chopped
1 Tbsp. saffron threads
½ cup dry white wine
3 egg yolks
¾ cup cream
Hot rice

Combine wing tips, necks and backs of chicken along with parsley, quartered onion, water and salt and pepper to taste. Simmer 1½ hours, then strain. Set aside 2½ cups broth.

In skillet, brown remaining chicken in olive oil. Cover and cook 50 minutes. Remove chicken to heated platter and add chopped onion, shallots and saffron to skillet. Stir briefly, then add wine and 2½ cups broth. Bring to a boil, then reduce to a simmer.

Beat egg yolks lightly and stir in the cream. Add a little hot broth to the yolk mixture, then stir mixture into simmering sauce, stirring briskly with wire whisk. Return chicken to sauce and serve with hot rice.

Chimbos
(small game birds with garlic and parsley sauce)
Serves 3

3 small game birds, skinned and cleaned
½ cup Spanish olive oil
½ cup minced onion
1 Tbsp. minced garlic
¼ cup minced Italian parsley
¼ tsp. salt
1 Tbsp. white wine vinegar
½ cup dry bread crumbs
1/3 cup dry white wine

Soak birds in water to cover, to which 1 tsp. salt has been added, for several hours. Drain and pat dry. Cut birds in half.

Heat olive oil in large Dutch oven over moderately high heat until a light haze forms. Add birds and brown, turning frequently. Remove birds to a heated platter when they have reached desired doneness. Add onion to pan drippings and cook a few minutes until wilted. Add remaining ingredients and cook 5 to 6 minutes. Pour over birds and serve at once.

Confit d'Oie
(preserved goose in its own fat)

8½ to 9½ lb. fresh goose
1¾ lb. goose fat
¾ lb. pork fat
1½ cups kosher salt
4 bay leaves, broken
3 Tbsp. fresh thyme leaves
3 tsp. freshly ground pepper
1 tsp. freshly grated nutmeg
¼ tsp. freshly ground cloves
15 garlic cloves, peeled

Cut up goose, cutting thighs and back into two parts, and breast into four. Remove wing tips and set aside. (Save for stock or soup.)

Put fat (goose and pork) into large Dutch oven with ½

cup water and cook on low heat until all fat has rendered. Discard scraps.

Mix together salt, herbs, and spices (excluding garlic). Rub goose pieces with salt mixture, using entire amount. Put pieces in heavy plastic bag, close tightly, and refrigerate for 2 days, turning bag often.

Remelt fat. Wipe goose pieces dry and put them in the melted fat in Dutch oven. Add garlic and weight meat down with heavy plate. Put Dutch oven on very low heat and cook very slowly for 1½ hours.

Pour 1 inch of cooking fat into the bottom of a clean dry crock and allow fat to harden. Pack partly cooled pieces of goose into crock and then strain cooking fat over pieces. A thick layer of fat should cover the pieces of goose and there should be no air spaces between meat pieces. Cover tightly and refrigerate. Keeps up to 1 year.

A piece of confit (with a little of the fat) is good added to a stew or casserole as a flavor booster. It is also good served, in small portions, warmed over low heat, and poured over mashed potatoes or rice.

Polla a la Vasca
Serves 4

2/3 cup Spanish olive oil
3 lbs. chicken, cut-up
Salt and pepper
3 cloves garlic, crushed
1 onion, chopped
2 ripe tomatoes, seeded and chopped
3 medium-sized sweet red peppers, peeled, seeded, and cut into strips
3 medium-sized green peppers, peeled, seeded, and cut into strips
1/3 lb. lean ham, cubed
1 cup dry white wine
½ lb. fresh mushrooms, sliced
½ cup chopped Italian parsley

Rub chicken with salt, pepper, and garlic. Brown in olive oil. Add onion, tomatoes, peppers, and ham. Stir in wine and mushrooms; cook over low heat until sauce has thickened. Add chopped parsley and serve at once.

Chukar, Basque Style
Serves 2 to 3

4 chukar breasts, skinned
Salt and pepper
4 strips of bacon
4 fresh grape leaves
    (bottled, if fresh unavailable)
¼ cup Spanish olive oil
2 medium onions, sliced
4 carrots halved and sliced lengthwise
1 lemon, cut into wedges
1 cup dry white wine
10 Spanish olives, pitted

Dry breasts and sprinkle with salt and pepper. Place in roasting pan and lay a strip of bacon over each breast. Cover each with a grape leaf. Sprinkle with olive oil. Surround leave covered breasts with onions, carrots, and lemon wedges. Bake in 350°F oven for 25 minutes. Remove grape leaves and bake 20 minutes longer, basting with pan drippings. Add wine and bake 10 minutes longer.

Place breasts on hot platter, surround with the cooked vegetables, and pour pan drippings over all. Garnish with Spanish olives.

Doves with Chiles and Sweet Peppers
Serves 4 to 5

10 dove breasts
½ cup Spanish olive oil
2 green Ancho chiles, chopped
2 sweet red peppers, seeded
    and cut into 1 inch strips
2 cloves garlic, chopped
½ cup tomato sauce
2 tsp. chopped Italian parsley
2 tsp. fresh oregano
White wine

Sprinkle breasts with salt and pepper. In skillet brown breasts in oil. Add onion, chiles, red peppers and garlic. Cook, stirring, for 2 minutes. Add remaining ingredients and enough wine to cover. Put lid on skillet and let breasts simmer for 1½ hours. Serve with hot rice.

Roast Duck with Chorizo Rice
Serves 5 to 6

2 2½ to 3 lb. ducks
2 cloves garlic, minced
Salt and freshly ground pepper
Zest of 2 lemons
¼ cup lemon juice
1 cup uncooked long grain white rice
2 Tbsp. Spanish olive oil
¼ lb. chorizo
1 medium-sized carrot, grated
1 medium-sized onion, chopped
¼ lb. lean ham, cut into 1 inch pieces
3 Tbsp. fresh lime juice
½ cup finely minced Italian parsley

Rub minced garlic over ducks and sprinkle with salt and pepper. Place lemon zest in cavities of ducks. Sprinkle ducks with lemon juice. Roast, uncovered, breast-side up, in 450°F oven for 20 minutes. Reduce heat to 350°F and roast for 2 hours, basting occasionally.

Cook rice according to instructions on package.

Cut chorizo into ¼ inch thick rounds and brown in olive oil. Add carrot and onion and cook until onion is transparent and soft. Add ham and cook 3 minutes longer. Stir in rice, 6 Tbsp. parsley, and lime juice.

Transfer duck to platter; skim fat from juices in pan. Add ½ cup water and boil over high heat, scraping pan, until liquid is reduced to ½ cup.

Spread rice mixture in shallow casserole. Carve duck and arrange on rice. Spoon sauce over all and sprinkle with remaining parsley. Serve at once.

Sage Hen
with Peppers, Tomatoes, and Olives
Serves 4

2½ to 3 lb. sage hen, cut into pieces
1 tsp. coarse salt
3 crushed green peppercorns
¼ cup Spanish olive oil
2 large onions, cut into strips
1 cup prosciutto ham, finely chopped
2 green peppers, cut into strips
2 sweet red peppers, cut into strips
6 medium-sized tomatoes, quartered
8 pitted black olives, halved
6 pitted green olives, halved

Sprinkle hen with crushed peppercorns and salt. Heat oil in skillet over high heat until light haze forms. Reduce heat and brown hen, a few pieces at a time. Transfer to plate.

Add onions, peppers and ham to remaining fat in skillet, stirring frequently. Cook until vegetables are soft, but not brown. Add tomatoes, raise the heat, and cook until liquid in pan evaporates.

Return sage hen to skillet, turning to coat in sauce. Cover tightly and simmer over low heat for 30 to 35 minutes. Stir in olives and serve at once.

Eggs

A house without fire is a body without blood.

Basque Proverb

Basque Eggs with Asparagus
Serves 4

2 medium-sized ripe tomatoes, chopped
¼ cup Spanish olive oil
¼ cup chopped green onions
1 Tbsp. minced garlic
1 green pepper, seeded, and finely chopped
4 oz. chorizo, sliced
2 Tbsp. chopped Italian parsley
¼ tsp. salt
2 tsp. olive oil
6 eggs
½ cup fresh peas
   (frozen, if fresh unavailable)
8 fresh asparagus, cooked and kept warm
¼ cup dry sherry
Italian parsley sprigs

Heat oil in heavy 12 inch skillet over medium heat until light haze begins to form. Add green onions, garlic, and green pepper, and cook 5 minutes.

Stir in chorizo, tomatoes, parsley, and salt. Boil briskly until most of the liquid has evaporated.

Preheat oven to 400°F. Coat bottom and sides of a 9×9″ baking dish with 2 tsp. olive oil. Spread chorizo sauce evenly in dish. Break eggs into dish arranging attractively atop the sauce. Arrange asparagus in parallel rows and scatter peas across sauce. Sprinkle with sherry and bake for 25 minutes. Garnish with parsley sprigs and serve at once.

Gypsy Eggs
Serves 4

1 medium-sized green pepper,
    seeded and chopped
½ cup chopped onion
2½ Tbsp. Spanish olive oil
2 Tbsp. tomato puree
3 Tbsp. grated goat cheese
Salt and freshly ground pepper
6 eggs
1/3 cup cream

Heat oil over medium-high heat until a light haze forms. Reduce heat to medium and saute green pepper and onion until wilted. Add tomato puree and cheese. Season to taste.

Beat together eggs and cream. Add to pepper mixture; cook and stir until eggs are set and fluffy.

Pisto Bilbaino
Serves 4

6 eggs, well beaten
3 Tbsp. Spanish olive oil
½ cup diced lean ham
½ cup sliced small zucchini
¼ cup chopped onion
½ cup green pepper,
    seeded, peeled, and chopped
1 medium tomato, chopped
Salt and pepper

Heat oil in heavy 12 inch skillet until light haze forms. Add ham and vegetables; cook until vegetables are tender. Season to taste with salt and pepper. Add eggs and cook over moderately low heat until eggs are set.

Potato, Chorizo, and Asparagus Omelet
Serves 6

1¼ cup Spanish olive oil
2 lbs. russet potatoes, peeled and
    sliced into ⅛ inch rounds
½ lb. asparagus, cut into 3 inch
    pieces and lightly steamed
½ cup finely chopped onion
¼ lb. chorizo, sliced
6 large eggs

In 12 inch skillet heat 1 cup olive oil over high heat until a light haze forms. Add potatoes and turn to coat in oil. Reduce to moderate heat and cook potatoes for 10 minutes, turning occasionally; then add onion and cook 10 minutes longer. Pour potato mixture into colander to drain excess oil.

Saute sliced chorizo in dry skillet until lightly browned. Set aside.

Whisk eggs until frothy. Gently stir in chorizo, potatoes and onion. Heat remaining ¼ cup oil in 12 inch skillet until a light haze forms. Pour in egg mixture and spread it out with a spatula. Arrange steamed asparagus on egg mixture. Cook over moderate heat for 3 to 4 minutes. Shake pan occasionally to keep eggs from sticking. When omelet is firm, cover with flat plate and invert skillet. Carefully slide omelet from plate back into skillet and cook 2 to 3 minutes longer. Serve at once.

Sheep Wagon Omelet
Serves 2

1 cup prepared lamb fries (see index)
2 Tbsp. chopped green pepper
2 Tbsp. chopped onion
1 clove minced garlic
2½ Tbsp. Spanish olive oil
1 Tbsp. minced Italian parsley
4 eggs, beaten
Salt and freshly ground pepper to taste

Heat oil in 12 inch cast iron skillet until light haze forms. Add green pepper, onion, and garlic; saute until vegetables wilt. Sprinkle parsley over vegetables. Pour eggs over vegetables in skillet and cook until eggs are set. Season with salt and pepper. Add lamb fries and fold omelet in half. Slide onto warm plate.

Desserts and Other Treats

*Women, gold, and linen should only be
chosen in daylight.*

Basque Proverb

Almond Cake

2 Tbsp. softened butter
2 Tbsp. flour
6 eggs, separated
¾ cup sugar
1 cup almond paste
¼ cup almonds, blanched and roasted
1 tsp. almond extract
1¼ cups sugar
1/3 cup water
10 egg yolks

Preheat oven to 350°F.

Oil an 11×17″ jelly roll pan with 1 Tbsp. soft butter. Line with waxed paper. Brush remaining butter over paper. Sprinkle flour evenly over paper and knock off excess.

Beat egg whites until soft peaks form. In separate bowl beat 6 yolks and ¾ cup sugar until thick and light colored. Stir in almond paste and extract.

Mix ¼ of the beaten whites into yolks, then pour over the remaining whites and gently fold together with rubber spatula. Pour into prepared pan and spread out evenly. Bake on middle rack for 20 minutes. Cool 2 to 3 minutes, then turn on fresh piece of waxed paper and cool cake to room temperature.

Combine sugar and water and cook over medium heat until sugar is dissolved. When translucent remove from heat and cool to room temperature.

Beat 10 egg yolks until thick and light yellow. Beating constantly, pour in syrup in thin steady stream. Place pan on lowest heat and cook, stirring with wooden spoon, until mixture is thick and coats spoon heavily. Strain and cool to room temperature.

Trim crusts from edges with a large, sharp knife and slice cake crosswise into four 11×4″ rectangles. Place one on serving plate and spread ¼ cup icing evenly over top. Set second layer on top and repeat procedure until all four layers have been stacked and iced. Ice sides of cake. Garnish with blanched and roasted almonds.

Almond Paste
1½ cups

6 oz. blanched almonds
2 Tbsp. honey
1½ tsp. almond extract
2½ egg whites

In food processor pulverize almonds. Place in bowl and mix with remaining ingredients.
Store in covered container. Keeps up to 1 month refrigerated.

Apple Crisp with Mint
Serves 6

Softened butter
1 cup sugar
1 cup whole wheat flour
½ tsp. baking powder
1 large egg
2 Tbsp. finely minced fresh mint
1 Tbsp. ground cinnamon
2 lbs. tart apples, peeled, quartered
    and cut into ¼ inch slices
2 cups of whipped cream

Butter sides and bottom of an 8″ square baking dish.
Sift together sugar, flour and baking powder into bowl. Make well in center and drop in egg. Mix together with 2 knives or pastry cutter until flour has absorbed the egg.
Stir together mint and cinnamon. Add apples and toss to mix well. Arrange slices in buttered pan. Scatter flour mixture over top, pressing it gently into a smooth layer to cover apples completely.
Bake at 350°F for 45 to 50 minutes. Serve at room temperature with whipped cream.

Arroz con Leche
Serves 6

4 cups milk
1/3 cup short-grained white rice
½ cup sugar
6 egg yolks
½ tsp. ground cinnamon
½ cup dried currants
1/3 cup sugar

In saucepan cook rice in milk over low heat for 35 minutes, stirring frequently. Add ½ cup sugar and cook another 30 minutes.

Cool to room temperature. Meanwhile carmelize 1/3 cup sugar in flan pan. Stir yolks, cinnamon and currents into rice. Spoon into flan pan. Place flan pan into larger pan with 1½ cups water and bake at 350°F for 40 to 45 minutes.

Chill. Loosen from mold and invert on platter.

Banana-Almond Cake

2/3 cup softened butter
2½ cups white pastry flour
1 2/3 cups sugar
1¼ tsp. baking powder
1 tsp. baking soda
½ tsp. salt
1½ cups mashed ripe banana
2/3 cup buttermilk
2 eggs
1 cup sliced toasted almonds
Brown sugar frosting (recipe follows)

Beat together butter, flour, sugar, baking soda, baking powder, and salt. Add bananas and 1/3 cup buttermilk; mix until flour is dampened. Beat for 2 minutes.

Add remaining buttermilk and 2 eggs. Beat well. Fold in toasted almonds. Bake in two paper-lined 9" round pans in 350°F oven for 35 minutes. Cool 10 minutes in pans. Remove; cool. Frost with Brown Sugar Frosting.

Brown Sugar Frosting

½ cup butter, melted
1 cup brown sugar
¼ cup hot milk
3¼ to 3½ cups confectioners sugar

Combine butter and brown sugar in saucepan and bring to boiling. Cook and stir 1 minute until slightly thickened. Cool 15 minutes. Add milk and beat until smooth. Beat in confectioners sugar until spreading consistency. Frost cake immediately.

Banana Fritters

1/3 cup confectioners sugar
1½ tsp. ground cardamon
2 cups flour
2½ tsp. baking powder
½ tsp. salt
2 Tbsp. softened butter
1 cup mashed ripe banana
Water
Peanut oil

Combine sugar with cardamon and set aside.

Sift together flour, baking powder and salt. Cut in butter until it resembles coarse meal. Stir in bananas and enough water to make a soft dough (approximately 5 to 6 Tbsp.). Knead dough on lightly floured surface until smooth. Roll out to ⅛ inch thickness on floured surface. Cut into 3 inch squares and cover with damp cloth.

Heat 3 inches of oil to 375°F. Fry squares for 1 minute, turning once. Drain on paper towels and sprinkle with cardamon/ sugar mixture.

Buttermilk Churros
(fried pastry puffs)
Makes 20

½ cup buttermilk
½ cup water
3 Tbsp. granulated sugar
½ cup butter
1 cup all purpose flour
4 eggs
2 tsp. pure vanilla extract
Lard for deep frying
½ tsp. ground cardamon seed
¼ tsp. freshly grated nutmeg
¾ cup granulated sugar

In large saucepan combine buttermilk, ½ cup water, 3 Tbsp. sugar, and butter. Bring to a boil over moderate heat. Add flour all at once and beat vigorously with spoon until a smooth batter forms.

With an electric mixer beat in eggs, one at a time. Beat in vanilla. Spoon dough into pastry bag fitted with a ½ inch star tip.

In Dutch oven heat lard to 375°F. Fat should be between 2 to 2½ inches deep. Pipe a few 4 inch lengths of dough into fat; fry, turning frequently until golden brown. Drain on paper towels, then toss with a mixture of ¾ cup sugar, nutmeg and cardamon. Fry remaining dough in same manner. Best eaten warm.

Basque Wedding Cookies
(4 dozen)

1 cup butter
¼ cup sifted confectioners sugar
1½ Tbsp. grated lemon peel
1 Tbsp. water
2½ cups sifted all purpose flour
2/3 cup whole blanched almonds
¾ cup confectioners sugar

Cream butter until light and fluffy. Stir in ¼ cup confectioners sugar, peel and water.

Mix flour with salt and beat into butter mixture. Knead with hands until dough is light. Pinch off heaping teaspoonsful of dough, press them flat and wrap around a whole almond to cover completely. Shape like a tiny leaf and place 1 inch apart on greased baking sheet. Bake at 350°F for 15 minutes. Take care not to overbake.

Remove from cookie sheet, cool 2 or 3 minutes, then roll in confectioners sugar. Cool completely, then roll again.

Flan
Serves 6

2 whole allspice
6 whole cloves
1 cinnamon stick
2 tsp. pure vanilla extract
1/3 cup sugar
6 eggs
6 Tbsp. sugar
2 cups milk

Tie spices in cheesecloth bag and place in milk to which vanilla has been added. Heat slowly. Beat together eggs and 6 Tbsp. sugar.

Carmelize 1/3 cup sugar over medium heat in flan pan. Slowly beat heated milk (spices removed) into beaten egg. Pour into flan pan. Place in container of water to reach edge of pan. Bake at 350°F for 20 minutes. Chill 6 hours or overnight. Unmold.

Flan de Castanas
Serves 8

2 lbs. chestnuts, roasted,
  peeled and mashed
2 cups sweetened condensed milk
1 tsp. pure vanilla extract
5 egg whites
1/3 cup sugar
Whipped cream

Mix mashed chestnuts with milk, egg whites, and vanilla.

Pour sugar in flan pan and carmelize over medium-high heat. Pour chestnut mixture over carmelized sugar. Place flan pan in larger pan containing 1½ inches hot water. Bake at 350°F for 30 minutes. Cool. Chill 6 hours.

Loosen mold and invert on serving platter. Serve with whipped cream.

Meringue Eggs
Serves 6

8 egg whites, slightly beaten
2/3 tsp. cream of tartar
¼ tsp. salt
2 cups fine granulated sugar
2 tsp. lemon juice
1½ tsp. vanilla extract
Whipped cream
Strawberry Sauce (recipe follows)

Beat whites with cream of tartar. Slowly beat in sugar and lemon juice. When stiff, fold in vanilla.

Lightly oil a tablespoon. Dip in meringue mixture and turn onto brown paper to form half egg shapes. Bake at 275°F for 1½ hours. Cool. Put halves together with whipped cream and place in serving dishes. Top with strawberry sauce.

Strawberry Sauce

6 cups whole ripe strawberries
4 cups sugar
3 Tbsp. lemon juice
½ tsp. finely grated lemon rind

Hull ripe strawberries. Crush berries with 2 cups sugar; add juice and rind. Simmer 3 minutes. Add remaining sugar and simmer 3 minutes longer. Skim and allow to cool overnight. Serve over meringue eggs.

Meringue Shells with Stewed Figs
Serves 8

6 egg whites
½ tsp. cream of tartar
⅛ tsp. salt
2 cups fine granulated sugar
2 tsp. freshly squeezed lemon juice
1 tsp. pure vanilla extract
Stewed Figs (recipe follows)

Beat whites until foamy; add cream of tartar and salt. Continue beating until whites begin to thicken, then slowly add sugar, ¼ cup at a time. When 1 cup sugar has been beaten in, add lemon juice and vanilla; continue beating until remaining sugar has been added and meringue is stiff.

Cut two 8 inch circles of brown paper. Spread meringue evenly in circles. Draw up slightly around edges. Bake in 275°F oven for 1½ hours. Cool. Fill with stewed figs.

Stewed Figs

36 fresh figs
½ cup water
Juice of 1 lemon
Zest of 1 lemon
1 Cassia bud
6 cloves
½ cup honey

Combine water, lemon juice, zest, cassia, and cloves in saucepan and bring to boiling. Add figs and cover. Reduce heat and simmer 7 to 10 minutes. Gently turn figs in syrup, then transfer drained figs to meringue shells. Chill.

Natilla
(Basque soft custard)
Serves 6

3 cups light cream
3 four inch cinnamon sticks
4 large eggs
2 egg yolks
2/3 cup sugar
Ground cinnamon

In 1½ quart saucepan heat milk with cinnamon sticks over medium heat until small bubbles form around edges of pan. Remove from heat. Set aside.

Beat together eggs, yolks, and sugar until pale yellow and slightly thickened. Remove cinnamon from milk. Beating constantly, slowly pour in the hot milk in a slow, steady stream. Return mixture to saucepan. Stirring constantly, cook over low heat until custard thickens enough to thinly coat the spoon. Do not allow custard to overheat or mixture will curdle. Cool to room temperature.

Serve by spooning into 6 custard cups and sprinkling with ground cinnamon.

Pastel Vasco
(Basque cream-filled pastry)
Serves 6

1½ cups plus 2 Tbsp. cake flour, sifted
½ cup sugar
½ cup softened butter
2 egg yolks
1¼ tsp. baking powder
2 tsp. grated lemon peel
Pastry cream (recipe follows)
Beaten egg

Put flour in bowl. Add sugar, butter, egg yolks, baking powder, and lemon peel. With finger tips, work into dough. Divide dough in half and roll each into a 9½ inch round. Place one in greased 9" spring form pan, shaping dough against sides. Fill center with pastry cream. Cover with other crust. Brush top with beaten egg. Cut diamond pattern on top crust.

Bake at 375°F (preheated) for 35 minutes.

Pastry Cream

1 cup sugar
7 egg yolks
1/3 cup flour
2 cups cream
1 tsp. almond extract
2 Tbsp. black cherry preserves

Beat together sugar and egg yolks until creamy and light colored. Add flour and mix just to combine.

Heat cream to lukewarm. Add cream, little by little, to yolk mixture, mixing well. Pour into saucepan and cook, stirring briskly, until mixture begins to thicken. Strain. Add extract and preserves. Cool.

Poor Man's Riches

6 egg yolks, slightly beaten
3 Tbsp. heavy cream
3 Tbsp. sugar
1 1/3 cups sifted all purpose flour
¼ tsp. salt
¼ tsp. ground cardamon seed
Hot fat or shortening for deep-fat frying
Confectioners sugar

Beat together yolks, cream, and sugar until well blended. Sift together flour, salt, and cardamon seed. Stir well, then knead slightly to make mixture smooth. Chill dough for 1 hour. Roll out to ⅛ inch thickness between 2 sheets of waxed paper. Cut into strips 4 inches long and 1½ inches wide. Slit one end of the dough and draw opposite side through.

Heat 2 inches of fat to 375°F and deep fry pieces of dough until delicate brown on each side. Drain on paper towels. Sprinkle with confectioners sugar while still warm. Cool. Store in airtight containers.

Zurrakapote
(Basque fruit compote)
Serves 6

3 cups dry white wine
1½ cups sugar
1 tsp. ground cinnamon
1 tart apple, peeled, cored, and sliced
1 ripe pear, peeled, cored, and sliced
1 cup dried apricots
1 cup dried pitted prunes
½ cup dried currants

In large saucepan bring wine and sugar to a simmer. Add cinnamon and apple; cook 10 minutes. Add remaining ingredients and cook 10 minutes longer. Allow to sit at room temperature overnight.

Misc

Almond Garlic Sauce

½ cup lightly toasted blanched almonds
2 tsp. finely chopped garlic
1/3 cup red wine vinegar
1 ripe tomato, peeled, seeded and
　　finely chopped
1 cup Spanish olive oil

In food processor, puree almonds and garlic. Add vinegar and tomato and whirl until ingredients are combined. Slowly beat in oil, 1 tablespoon at a time. The sauce will hold its shape solidly in a spoon.

Store in covered container in the refrigerator. Serve with shellfish or chicken.

Baked Boletus Custard
Serves 4 to 5

2 lbs. Boletus edulus mushrooms,
　　spores removed
¼ cup butter
¼ cup all purpose flour
1¼ cups milk
½ cup light cream
½ tsp. salt
¼ tsp. pepper
3 egg yolks
3 egg whites

Slice Boletus and put in large heavy skillet. Cook over moderate heat until most of the liquid has been cooked out. Chop mushrooms and set aside.

Melt butter in saucepan. Gradually add flour and cook 1 minute. Stir in milk, cream, salt, and pepper. Cook until thickened.

Beat egg yolks; add some of the cream sauce to yolks, then add yolks to the rest of the sauce. Beat whites stiff and fold into sauce. Fold in mushrooms and spoon mixture into mold greased with butter.

Place mold into baking dish which has been half-filled with hot water. Bake in 350°F oven for 40 to 45 minutes, or until knife comes out clean when inserted.

Garlic Mayonnaise

3 egg yolks
1½ Tbsp. fresh lime juice
½ Tbsp. good quality mustard
8 cloves garlic
1 cup peanut oil
½ cup extra-virgin olive oil

In food processor, mix yolks, lime juice, mustard, and garlic until smooth. With machine running, add the oils in a slow steady stream. Continue processing until thick. Store in glass container, refrigerated. Keeps 3 weeks.

Limonada
(red and white wine beverage)

6 lemons
2 limes
2 cups fine sugar
1 liter dry red wine
1 liter dry white wine

Remove zest from 3 lemons and 1 lime. Cut zest into 2 inch long strips. Set aside.

Squeeze juice from peeled lemons and lime, then slice remaining lemons and limes into ¼ inch thick rounds, discarding ends. Combine strips of zest, lemon and lime juice, lemon and lime slices, and sugar in large serving pitcher. Pour the red and white wine in, stir well and chill at least 8 hours, stirring several times.

Fill tumblers with ice cubes and add limonada.

Cuajada
(milk curds)

Add ⅛ cake yeast to 1 cup warm ewe's milk. Let stand covered in warm place for 24 hours. Pour off half liquid and add 1 cup warm ewe's milk. Each day for seven days pour off half the liquid and add 1 cup warm ewe's milk. On the seventh day do not drain off any milk, but add 2 cups warm ewe's milk. Let stand 24 hours. This makes three cups cultured starter for cheese or yogurt.

Bring 1 gallon ewe's milk to 75-80°F. Add 1 cup cultured starter. Cover and let stand in warm place for 24 hours.

Cut clabber into cubes, then set container into larger pot containing warm water. Warm curds to 110°F, stirring often. Do not over-heat.

Pour into strainer lined with cheesecloth and drain for a few minutes. Lift cheesecloth from strainer and rinse under tepid running water to rinse off whey. Place in dish and salt to taste. Chill.

Roasted Red or Green Peppers

Broil peppers on the rack of broiler pan under broiler 2 inches from heat. Turn peppers every 5 minutes until skins are blistered and charred (approximately 20 minutes).

Place peppers in plastic bag and let steam until cool enough to handle. Peel, beginning at bottom ends. Cut off tops and discard seeds.

Lore

Satisfy a dog with a bone; a woman with a lie.

Basque Proverb

Introduction

As a young girl I spent a great deal of time riding my burro—and, in later years, my horse—out across the sagebrush near my parents' home in McCall, Idaho. Herds of sheep passed through there in the spring and autumn of each year. I was always fascinated by the herders of these bands; many of them spoke little or no English at all. I was equally fascinated by the fragrance of rich stews and hearty breads which mingled with the pungent odor of sagebrush at day's end. As a child I never thought much about the reasons for the Basques being there. They had always been there, as far as I knew, and were a part of the over-all picture of my youth.

As an adult, however, I became more interested in the Basques. The literature I read concerning them was detailed as to their background and culture, but left me unsated in a curious sort of way. I hungered for a more personal glimpse of their character. I set out to gather information which would more clearly show the personalities of these interesting people. I also began collecting Basque recipes since this, too, was part of the nostalgia of my childhood memories.

I have had a lot of help along the way, both from written accounts and from oral tattle-taling. I am especially grateful to the tattle-talers, some Basque, some not, who shared their stories with me. One fact became very clear in my research: Basques love to tattle on themselves!

Putting this information together was not unlike piecing together a patch-worked quilt. A lot of material was set aside unused, not because it was not good, but because it wouldn't work into the pattern which I was attempting to create.

This is by no means a history of a people. Several well-written histories already exist. This is a mosaic of personalities and flavors—Basque cooking and lore of the West.

Bull

During the late 1920s, a Basque Jordan Valley cattle rancher decided to upgrade his herd. He had been eyeing an award-winning bull wearing a $2,000 price tag. After careful consideration, the rancher purchased the pricey bull.

From the onset there seemed to be a smart aleck side to the bull which the Basque rancher found disconcerting. The first time he put the bull with the cows, the beast took one look at the bovine lot and jumped the four foot fence to freedom.

The Basque felt defensive about the bull's action. After all, the cows were the best from his herd and the high-priced bull seemed to think himself superior.

So the rancher added another foot to his fence and led the bull back in among the cows. With not a sniff of interest the bull sprang over the five foot fence, then paused a moment to peer over his shoulder at the angry rancher.

The Basque later swore that he saw the bull snicker, though this drew snorts of disbelief from those who heard the tale.

Not to be defeated, the Basque added yet another foot to his fence. He returned the $2,000 bull to the cows. The bull looked at the cud-chewing group a moment, then with the flick of his tail went over the six foot fence. He paused to look over his shoulder at the irate Basque. It was the last look—or snicker, as the rancher described it—that the bull ever had. The Basque dropped the bull in his tracks with one well-placed bullet.

Elorriaga's House

In 1911, a man named Elorriaga came to this country from the Pyrenees to work sheep in Jordan Valley. The harsh dryness of the high desert was in stark contrast to the green mountains of his homeland. Like so many Basques, Elorriaga adapted to the change and worked hard. He soon made the money needed to bring his wife and two daughters from the Pyrenees to Jordan Valley. His wife, however, had heard rumors about the Wild West. She didn't relish the thought of her two little girls being consumed by ravenous bears or of her own scalp dangling from some Indian's war pony. Though Elorriaga tried to explain through his letters that period in his new country's history had come to an end, his wife continued to believe the worst. She felt safe in her large ancestral stone house in the Pyrenees and wished to remain embraced in that secure feeling. However, in spite of her fears, Elorriaga's wife was not an unfair woman. She let it be known that if Elorriaga built a replica of her Pyrenees home, she would feel relatively safe within its stone walls.

Elorriaga was crest-fallen. The construction of such a vast stone building seemed improbable. Fellow Basques in the area noticed his down-trodden nature and goaded him into confiding his troubles. Word of Elorriaga's plight spread and soon Basques from miles around began arriving to help Elorriaga build his house.

Stone was quarried from the nearby mountains and hauled by wagon to the new homesite. Men toiled for months, working from plans of the ancestral home Elorriaga sketched from memory. When the house was completed it was clearly the largest, sturdiest, and most beautiful home in the valley.

Rupert's Sheep Dog Business

Good sheep dogs were a necessity in the sheep business, but were often difficult to obtain. When properly trained, the dogs would help guide the sheep in the direction the herder wished them to go. A good dog also kept close vigil at night and would alert the herder when anything was amiss. Scotch collies and Australian shepherds were the most sought after dogs, but mixed breeds often made good sheep dogs, too.

Since camptenders, traveling from town to town and camp to camp, were more mobile than the sheepherders, they kept an eye open for any dog they thought might make a good sheep dog. They would bargain with the dog's owner and, if successful, deliver the new acquisition to one of the sheep camps.

Rupert Niece was a nine-year-old lad whose family had a homestead in the lower end of Idaho's Sawtooth Valley around 1912. He owned a collie mix named Hero.

Hero was an intelligent-looking dog, quick to respond to commands. He had a respect for sheep, having grown up in an area where bands were prevalent. Hero drew the attention of a camptender passing through the homestead when he was little more than a pup. The silver dollar the camptender offered the little boy was too great a temptation to pass up. Holding the shiny coin in his palm eased some of the guilt Rupert felt as the camptender tied a rope around Hero's neck and led him away.

Two days later, to Rupert's glee, Hero loped up the trail, tongue lolling in the August heat, but as pleased as he could be that he had found his way home. Though the camptender returned for the dog, Hero returned home again two days later.

The following spring another Basque camptender spotted Hero and recognized a potential sheep dog. Again Rupert pocketed a shiny coin as he watched his dog being led away. Hero, of course, found his way home.

Thus, a profitable sheep dog business began for Rupert. He sold Hero again and again. Eventually news of the "homing dog" spread among the Basque sheep camps, but that didn't seem to slow Rupert's business much. The Basque camptenders and sheepherders rose to the challenge and wagered among themselves. Who would win the heart and loyalty of Hero?

Yet, as years went by, Hero remained true to Rupert. The journeys home, time and time again, were beginning to take their toll on aging Hero so Rupert decided that it was time for them to retire from the sheep dog business.

The Basque camptenders and sheepherders were disappointed to hear that Hero had been taken off the market.

Learning The Language

Domingo came to Mountain Home directly from the "Old Country." Unlike Boise, Mountain Home had not established its Basque community at that time. The small, dusty town squatting in the shadows of the Owyhee Mountain Range bore little resemblance to the lushness of Domingo's homeland. The arid vastness, the blue sage, and the jack rabbits brought to him no feelings of familiarity.

Domingo was of a hardy and determined people, and he resolved to make the best of his situation. Since language was the biggest obstacle, Domingo set about learning the tongue of this new land.

Not far from Domingo's dwelling stood a rustic eatery. Every evening around mealtime the fragrant cooking odors would draw Domingo to the establishment.

Gradually, Domingo was able to understand some of what was being said among the proprietors of the restaurant. He prided himself on this accomplishment until he discovered that he had not been picking up tidbits of the English language, but Chinese.

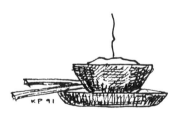

Chewing Gum

A young Basque arrived at New York via ship, then began the long journey west by train. The newness and adventure of his undertaking had worn thin and the young lad, a devout Catholic, began to feel homesick.

He thought of the opportunities the new land offered— an industrious lad such as himself could make enough money to return to his homeland a wealthy man. This was his dream, but in the face of all that was strange and unfamiliar, the dream had begun to turn stale.

The lad looked about him. Many of the passengers were chewing gum. Suddenly, he began to feel a kinship with these gum-chewing passengers, even though gum chewing was unknown to the Basque. At journey's end he wrote a glowing letter to his "ama." Included in his missive was the statement, "Mother, you need not worry. On the train ride west, I noticed many people reciting the rosary to themselves."

KP 91

Martin And The Mutton

In the early 1920s an old man named Martin lived in a shack at the edge of a small Idaho lake. Mount Borah loomed to the east and grass-covered slopes rolled west.

One summer's afternoon, Martin came upon two lads in their late teens camped not far from his abode. The boys had experienced car trouble and their vehicle was in a Mackay garage awaiting a new ring gear. The part was not due to arrive for two weeks. Since a storm was blowing in from Mount Borah, Martin invited the boys to share his cabin.

Now, Martin was a hermit of sorts, but he also enjoyed impressing others with his tales and anecdotes when opportunities arose. That first evening, as a summer thunderstorm raged, Martin entertained the boys into the wee hours of the morning.

The next morning, as Martin stood at the edge of his porch gazing out across the grassy slopes, he spied sheep in the distance. Instantly, the sly Martin seized the opportunity to show the boys that he was "king of the mountain."

"Those stinkin' mountain maggots!" he roared. "They ruin the country. Dirty up the creeks! Chew up the meadows! By God, I'll teach 'em a lesson about coming into my territory!"

Martin glanced through the open door to see what effect he was having on the boys. Sure enough, they were up and getting dressed, fearful that they might miss some action.

"Tell you what I'm going to do! I'm going to set off a charge that'll turn a whole mountain of rock on 'em. Bury the buzzards!" Martin stole another look at the boys, who were now bare-footing it out to the porch.

"I'm going down and tell that Basque Pedro to get his lice out of here pronto. If he doesn't, I'll break his neck before I blast the sheep!" Martin bellowed.

The old man took off down the hill armed with a shotgun and lots of ammunition. The two wide-eyed boys waited anxiously at the cabin. Martin returned that evening carrying half a lamb, which he slammed down on the plank table in his shack.

"Put the fear into Pedro!" he boasted. "Told him off good. He gave me this mutton so I wouldn't blow him up!"

The next day the boys made their exit, bidding old Martin farewell and thanking him for the shelter and the meals of lamb. They hiked down the grass-covered slopes and were surprised to come upon the Basque sheepherder playing his guitar. They boldly approached the Basque and asked him how he could be so brave as to stay around Martin's territory after being threatened in such a harsh manner.

"There is no trouble," the Basque answered. "Martin comes and tells me to go away. I tell him to go jump. We sit and drink lots of wine together. Good friends, now."

"Why did you give him the lamb?" They asked.

"Old man paid for the lamb. Said he had two hungry boys to feed." The herder tells them. "Then he gives me all the shotgun shells to shoot the coyotes that bother my sheep."

The Man Without A Shadow

There were three Basque brothers named Axular and all decided that they would take lessons from the Red Master—the devil. The Red Master agreed to teach the three brothers for one year and one day on one condition—that upon departure the last one out his door was to be kept as the Red Master's payment. The three brothers, so eager to learn, agreed, not hesitating to ponder which one out the door might be the last.

The year and one day passed quickly since the three brothers were so engrossed in learning all the mystical and magical lessons the devil taught them. The last night found each of the brothers unable to sleep, hoping that he was not going to be the last to exit the devil's domain. At daybreak the three lept from their cots and raced to the door, the two oldest ahead and the youngest behind.

The Red Master was waiting at the doorway for them as they raced through, grabbing the last—the youngest—and shouting, "My payment! The last one of you!"

The youngest Axular sprang aside and pointed to the shadow behind him. "Take that one," he said, "for he is the last."

The Red Master grabbed the shadow and young Axular scurried out the door. From that time on, Axular was known as "the man without a shadow" and was considered among the Basque to be a very wise man for having fooled the Red Master.

KP 91

Lambing Time — 1935

The dirt floor of the long, narrow, weathered wood-sided lambing shed has been swept clean. The gates on the twenty four stalls hang open on rusting hinges awaiting the arrival of the "drop band."

There are twelve stalls to the left of the center aisle and twelve to the right, each approximately sixteen feet wide by twelve feet deep. Along the walls are feeder boxes and four by two foot metal troughs for holding water.

Kerosene lanterns sway from the rafters, put into motion by the wind which forces its way in through the gaps in the old board siding.

At the west end of the long building is a large open area. Two tons of straw are stacked along the north wall. Along a portion of the west wall is a barrel stove. A similar stove is backed up near the east wall at the far end of the building. A couple of cords of split firewood are stacked near each.

An old wood cook stove graces the corner where the east and south walls meet. A Dutch oven sits on top. Above the stove spans two long, narrow plank shelves containing the lambing supplies.

There's a large box of baking soda, a five gallon crock of sourdough starter, a neatly folded stack of gunny sacks, a bushel basket filled with old whiskey and soft drink bottles, a funnel, a tin pail filled with rubber nipples, a bottle of cheap whiskey, a roll of jute, and a large tin of antiseptic balm.

There's also several gallons of thick, black sheep paint, one pint of white, some well-used heavy cotton gloves, and several small paint brushes. Several dusty bottles of mineral spirits are nearly obscured behind the gallons of paint.

Several bedrolls and old blankets appear to have been drop-kicked into the corner behind the cook stove.

At the west end of the building double doors swing wide to reveal the holding corrals. There's pasture beyond the corrals and a flock of around five hundred ewes nibble at the tiny shoots of new grass. The crisp wind whips away any warmth the early March sun may have intended to share, but the ewes in their thick wool coats don't seem to notice its absence.

Alfonso does. Down at the river he's filling fifty gallon drums with icy water and rolling them up planks into the back of the flatbed truck. The morning sun has yet to reach the shaded sandbar, and the wind blowing downriver carries with it a nasty sting.

A horse neighs and Alfonso looks up from his chore to see the Corta brothers, Pete and Domingo, ride across the pasture. They've come down from the upper canyon. The two have homes there. And families.

By the time Alfonso arrives at the lambing shed with the load of water-filled drums, Pete and Domingo have spread fresh straw on the hard-packed dirt floors of the stalls. Alfalfa hay from the outside stack fills the feeders. The three work together to fill the troughs with water from the barrels.

The flock of ewes are moved into the holding corrals. Several show no signs of pregnancy and are quickly separated and turned back into the pasture. The biggest, broadest, most uncomfortable ewes are herded through the double doors and into the stalls—ten to twelve ewes per stall. It will take several weeks for all the ewes to lamb, and it's a guessing game to pick those most likely to lamb first from those which will lamb later. The guessing game must be played since the shed will hold approximately one quarter of the pregnant flock at one time. The ewes in the holding corrals are fed and watered.

It has taken all day to prepare for the lambing. Pete and Domingo ride home in growing darkness.

Alfonso stays with the ewes. He builds a fire in the cook stove and prepares a simple Dutch oven meal of potatoes, rabbit, and carrots. Sourdough dumplings steam atop the stew.

The Basque eats his supper seated within a sphere of light cast by a kerosene lantern. As darkness fills the shed the din of bleating ewes tapers down to the baas of two or three chronic complainers. Alfonso is lost in his little circle of light, his thoughts not of the task before him, but of his girl, Maria, back home in Vizcaya. Feeling himself slipping into loneliness and longing, Alfonso returns to thoughts of the lambing.

He strolls along the center aisle, carrying the lantern, and checks the ewes in the stalls. The ewes mill around uneasily, stressed by the unfamiliarity of their surroundings. Alfonso goes outdoors into the holding corrals and checks the remaining flock.

Back in the shed he unrolls a bedroll and lays it on top of a pile of fresh straw. The smells of the sheep, fresh straw, and musty odor of the bedroll are vaguely comforting. This is Alfonso's third spring at the lambing shed and he views it as one of the highlights of being a sheepman.

Around three in the morning, Alfonso awakens. He reluctantly leaves the warmth of the bedroll. The cook stove is filled with a fresh supply of wood. The Basque shivers as he lights a lantern and makes the rounds. All's well inside, but when he checks the holding corral he finds a ewe has given birth.

The lamb lays encased in its placenta, its mother looking on with a blend of curiosity and confusion.

Alfonso quickly checks the mother, a young ewe experiencing her first birth. The ewe is fine, but the lamb has been lying unattended for a period of time. Alfonso tears away the placenta, places the still form beneath his coat, against the warmth of his body, and rushes to the east end of the building. He wraps the lamb in a gunny sack and places it on the opened door of the stove, then dampens down the flame, but the lamb dies. The dead animal is placed outside the holding corrals.

The rounds are made again. All is still. Alfonso returns to his bedroll.

He awakens at sunrise to the bleating of a newborn. In the fifth stall on the south side a ewe has delivered a pair of twins. Both are healthy and busily butting at the full udder of their patient mother.

Further down the row of stalls, Alfonso's experienced ear picks out the grunts of a ewe in labor. He checks the mother-to-be and all seems normal.

The flock in the holding corrals are hungrily milling around. Alfonso breaks open bales of alfalfa and tosses the hay to the ewes. In doing so he notices a suspect ewe. She isn't rushing to the feed with the flock. With some athletics and acrobatics, Alfonso manages to corner the now frantic ewe to check her udder. She shows milk. With a firm grip on her woolly neck and rump, Alfonso wrestles the struggling ewe into the lambing shed and stuffs her into one of the already crowded stalls.

Again he checks the twins and the ewe in labor, and in doing so, spots another ewe which appears to be in labor. A closer examination reveals stomach bloat. Apparently the ewe had consumed more than her share of the rich alfalfa hay. A dose of baking soda and water corrects the problem.

Alfonso makes himself a pot of coffee, and with cup in hand makes the rounds again. The ewe found in labor in the holding corrals earlier that morning has delivered a healthy lamb. Several more ewes have begun labor.

Alfonso spots one dangling a pair of hind legs—a breech birth. He jumps into the stall and corners the ewe. Alfonso manages to dislodge the lamb. Another follows, this time fore-feet and head first. The mother wants nothing to do with the pair. She's hurt and trembling from the difficult birth. Alfonso cleans the newborns and leaves them with their mother, hoping that she'll change her mind.

Meanwhile another ewe has delivered and happily cleans her youngster.

The sound of bells tinkles across the pasture. The Corta brothers have arrived, bringing with them eight milk goats. The goats are herded into a stall set aside for them. In the corner of the stall is a wooden milking platform. Hanging from the rafters are a dozen tin pails. The nannies are fed and watered, then Domingo begins the task of milking. Most of the goat's milk will not be used during the first few days of lambing, but an attempt will be made to keep it cold and fresh in kegs stored in the river. As more and more "bummers" accumulate, the milk will become more precious.

Alfonso checks on the ewe which has had the difficult birth. Her twins are standing in the corner of the stall shivering from the cold. Their mother is munching alfalfa, ignoring her offspring. Alfonso retrieves the first "bummers" of the season, carrying each under an arm, and calls to Domingo to bring some fresh goat's milk.

The two "bummers" are rubbed down with gunny sacks. Pete has built fires in both barrel stoves. An extra layer of straw is placed in the pen located closest to the east stove—the "bummer" pen.

Alfonso places the funnel in the top of an old whiskey bottle and pours in the warm milk, adding a couple of spoonfuls of sourdough starter to each to aid digestion, then tops the bottle with a rubber nipple.

The "bummers" reject the bottle. Alfonso squeezes a few drops of the milk on their lips, then rubs it across their teeth. Once they catch on to the idea they become eager feeders.

Pete comes rushing up from one of the stalls holding a stillborn. From far down the aisle the frantic calls of its mother fills the barn. The dead lamb is quickly skinned and the woolly little cape is draped over the stronger of the two "bummers" and tied into place with a couple of lengths of jute.

The frantic mother eyes the odd-looking four-legged form pushed at her by the hopeful Basque. Alfonso watches intently. The ewe sniffs the cape and recognizes the scent of her stillborn lamb. She begins making guttural sounds and the lamb sidles closer. Having not finished its breakfast, it begins nosing around and before long finds the sought after food. The union completed, Alfonso hop-skips back to the cook stove like an excited youngster. One less "bummer" to attend.

The lambing has begun in earnest. All three men are kept busy. Weak and chilled lambs have cheap whiskey spooned down their throats—and a few warming swallows find their way down the throat of the administering Basque. The lambs are then slid into gunny sacks and placed on the open door of the cook stove to warm. Most survive this treatment and are either returned to their mothers or to the "bummer" stall. Those which die, along with the few ewes that fail to survive the birthing, are rolled into a pit at day's end and covered with a layer of lime and straw.

As pregnant ewes are brought in from the holding corrals, the new mothers with the stronger lambs are turned out. Each ewe and offspring is painted with corresponding numbers. The dark sheep paint is easy to spot on the woolly white back and makes reunions easier in cases where mothers become separated from their youngsters. Any black lambs are marked with white paint. After the tails of the lambs are docked, their ears are notched with the owner's "brand."

So goes the day. Pete and Domingo settle in at the lambing shed for the duration. Their wives make two trips daily bringing hot food to the three working men. The lambs, to the Basque, are precious jewels and each is treated with the utmost care. The three brought from their homeland respect for the sheep and for the food and clothing they provide. To the sheepmen of the west, these foreign herders mean an increase in profits through better care of the stock.

and they were bunched and bedded down. Obviously they had fattened well on their range land, and were enroute to the stock yards to be weighed and sold.

From his viewpoint on the ridge Maness drew a deep breath and cut loose with a Pyrenees war cry—the irrintzi. To the cattle the Ai-ee-ee-ee-ee-ee! Ai-eeeeeee! shriek of the Basque must have sounded like the murderous whinny of some gigantic devil horse, for they stampeded.

Maness grinned as he watched the panic-stricken steers bolt up and over the first ridge, then the next, and then disappear from sight. He knew that the cattle could be rounded up easily enough, but there would be no way that the valuable pounds lost in the run could be replaced before shipping time.

Ascequinolasa And The Mother Bear

It was a warm spring day. The sheep grazed contentedly along the sunny slope of an Idaho hillside. Ascequinolasa shared breakfast with his blue-eyed sheep dog and thought of the placid day before him.

Suddenly the dog's ears jerked forward. Ascequinolasa looked up along the ridge and saw two black bear cubs having a sibling wrestling match. Before he could get a hand on the dog, the canine was off to join the fun. Shouting Basque profanities, Ascequinolasa raced after the dog, but his words went unheeded.

When the sheep dog reached the cubs, he began nipping at their heels. The cubs began wailing for their mother as they loped towards the nearest aspen tree and scaled up. The dog danced on his two hind legs barking joyfully.

Before Ascequinolasa could retrieve his erring dog, mother bear showed up and gave one long, accusing look at the innocent sheepherder before pursuing the terror-stricken man.

Like the cubs, Ascequinolasa sprinted for the nearest aspen tree with the angry mother bear hot on his heels. With uncanny agility, Ascequinolasa ascended the frail tree. The bear managed to slash the heel off the man's boot before he had shimmied out of reach.

The tree was a good and bad situation for the sheepherder: good due to the fact that it was too skinny for the bear to climb; bad because of its size. There were no limbs strong enough to support the man's weight.

Again Ascequinolasa called to his dog, hoping the animal would come away from the treed cubs and allow the three bears to vacate the area. However, the thrill-seeking dog ignored the man.

Time passed and the bear seemed as content as the dog to sit at the base of the tree and wait for its prey to either climb out or fall out.

Ascequinolasa's arms and legs ached from hugging the tree. He knew that it was only a matter of time before he fell to the jaws and claws of the bear. Then he noticed the long dry tufts of last year's grass at the base of the tree. Reaching into his jacket pocket, Ascequinolasa found a book of matches. It took great dexterity to light the matches while hugging the tree, but the sheepherder managed the feat. Time and time again he dropped a burning match onto the tufts of grass. Time and again the flame flickered out. Then, miraculously, some tufts flared and the flames began consuming the grass, working their way towards the bear.

Finding things no longer in her favor, the mother bear abandoned her post and swaggered over to the dog. One fierce slap at the yapping beast sent the canine somersaulting down the hill. The cubs descended the tree and the three disappeared over the rise.

Ascequinolasa summoned the trembling dog and the two stiffly made their way back to camp to have an early supper. From that day on the dog followed Basque reasoning—a sheepherder commands the dog; the dog commands its tail.

The Tree Of Guernica

Beneath the spreading branches of a gigantic oak tree, heads of each Euzkadi household met every two years to form laws governing their country. The tree was known as the Tree of Guernica. Though time eventually took its toll on the oak, its remains are now protected by a roof supported by majestic columns and encircled by an artistically decorated iron fence.

Basques from that province who emigrated to the United States never forgot the symbolic Tree of Guernica.

In 1980, a group of Idaho Basques formed a committee to obtain a seedling of the Tree of Guernica, to be planted in their adopted city of Boise—a reminder, for future generations, of their proud heritage. Members of the committee included Secretary of State Pete Cenarrusa, Joe Eiguren, Julian Archabal, Inake Eiguren, John Bastida, Nick Beristain, Julio Bilbao, Roy Eiguren, Justin Sarria, and Marie C. Totorica. Months of preparation and red tape followed.

Three seedlings were selected by the Forester General of Guernica. The Forester named the trees Jose, Jon, and Peter. In April of 1982, the young trees were air-freighted to Boise.

In the tradition of the Basque, a great celebration preceded the planting of the chosen seedling. On April 18, as Basque music played in the background, the seedling, Jon, was carried in a procession down the Statehouse steps to a stage assembled on the grounds between Basque and United States flags.

Members of the audience sang the song *Agur Jaunak.* Then Idaho's Catholic Bishop, His Excellency Sylvester Treinen, gave an invocation and blessed the seedling.

Alberto Amorrortu and Jose Manuel, Deputies of the Provincial Parliament of Vizcaya, presented the tree. Severiane Legaretta stepped forth to receive it.

Another song, *Gernika Arbola,* was sung, then John Evans, Idaho's Governor, officially accepted the seedling. Oinkari Basque Dancers performed the Ikurrina and Zortziko dances amid the clapping and cheering of the crowd, followed by the presentation of the Basque flag to the State of Idaho. Idaho Secretary of State Pete Cenarrusa made a closing statement before seedling Jon was planted in his place of honor.

The next morning it was discovered that Jon had been stolen and a scraggly branch had been left in Jon's place. Although a substantial reward was offered for the return of the young oak, no one came forth.

A year and a half later Jose was planted in Jon's place in an unBasque-like manner. There was neither gala celebration nor exorbitant fanfare to draw attention to Jose.

The Seven Mules

As Basque legend goes, there were two camptenders, Baptista and Michel, and each had seven mules. One day they made a bet and he who lost the bet turned his mules over to the other. Baptista won the wager and Michel lost his mules.

With the loss of his mules, Michel had no way to move the sheep camps, and therefore had lost his livelihood. He became very distraught and went for a long walk, stopping beneath a bridge for a drink of water from the stream. While drinking he overheard two witches talking:

"Baptista's wife, Marianna, has been ill for seven years and no one can cure her. She contemptuously threw a piece of holy bread out a church door and it landed in the mouth of a toad. She will die soon."

Michel hastened to the nearby village and inquired as to where Baptista's family lived. He thus approached the household and was greeted by Baptista's beautiful daughter, Maria.

"I must speak with your mother," Michel said. "It is urgent."

From the ailing woman Michel learned the location of the church, where, seven years ago, Marianna had angrily cast aside the holy bread. Though the journey was long, Michel went to the church. He lifted a large flat stone by the doorway. Beneath the stone sat a fat toad, still holding the holy bread in its mouth. Michel returned to Baptista's household and instructed the woman to eat the bread. Her cure was rapid and complete.

When Baptista heard of Michel's deed, he returned not only Michel's mules, but offered the man his beautiful daughter's hand in marriage, as well.

The Stolen Pig

When a Basque farmer kills a pig he makes chorizos to give to his friends, neighbors, and local priest. Rodrigo had only one pig, but being a generous man, made many sausages for his friends. He even took extra chorizos to the priest.

The priest thanked Rodrigo for the sausages, then asked the farmer for some advice. The priest was going to butcher his pig that afternoon, but it was only a small one—"and if I make sausage for all who have made sausages for me, there will be no pork left for my larder," the priest concluded.

Rodrigo looked at the priest, his eyes narrowed in thought. Then an idea came.

"Hang the carcass from your front porch for all to see. When it becomes dark tonight cut the pig down and hide it," Rodrigo whispered. "Then cry that the pig has been stolen!"

Sure enough, just after dark the priest began yelling, "My pig's been stolen! My pig's been stolen!"

Rodrigo ran to the priest and said in a low voice so that the gathering crowd could not hear, "That's the way, Father! That's the way!"

"But Rodrigo, my pig really *has* been stolen!" The priest exclaimed, wringing his hands.

"Wonderful acting," Rodrigo exclaimed. "I almost believed it myself!" Then he sauntered back to his farm. He had chorizos to make for his friends—even if it was a small pig.

Ranger Horton — In The Line Of Duty

In the early 1900s, Bill Horton was the Ranger for the Pole Creek Ranger Station near Idaho's Galena Summit by Sawtooth Valley.

The way over the summit was, at that time, a narrow, twisting, steep dirt road. Since over 80,000 sheep ranged in the region and had to be trailed over the summit in spring and fall, a sheep trail was built not far from the road.

One cold, rainy autumn day, as Ranger Horton was making his rounds, he came across a Basque herder trailing his band of sheep along the summit road heading to winter pasture near the Wood River area. The Ranger approached the herder and very diplomatically explained the dangers of trailing sheep along the treacherous public road versus the advantages of using the established sheep trail.

The herder looked at Horton, a blank expression on his face, and shrugged his shoulders.

In pantomime, Ranger Horton tried to convey his message to the uncomprehending Basque. Icy rain ran from the brim of Horton's hat and down the back of his neck as he made a sweeping hand gesture towards the band of sheep, then pointed to the trail on the ridge above the roadway.

Still the herder gave no indication that he understood any of what Horton was attempting to convey.

Not a man to give up, Ranger Horton tried to turn the sheep towards the trail. They ran this way and that as the inexperienced, self-appointed herder slipped to and fro trying to keep his footing on the slick muddy road. The Basque watched, an involuntary smile twitching his lips.

Finally the exhausted, mud-splattered Ranger got the sheep headed in the right direction. The difficult job of turning the sheep accomplished, the Basque herder fell in behind the band and helped usher them up the steep embankment of the trail.

Task completed, the cold, wet, tired Ranger turned to the Basque for a farewell shake of hands. The Basque, no longer able to contain his smile, broke into a broad grin, and said in clear English, "It sure don't rain here like it does in Oregon."

What Justice

The two buckaroos had been herding cattle down off the Owyhee range for ten days. On this particular autumn afternoon they had made camp in a ravine near Three Forks. The two men sat before the warmth of the sage-brush fire looking at the tiresome fare of beans and dried beef simmering in the Dutch oven. Neither sight nor odor of the cooking food whetted their appetites. Beans and dried beef for breakfast, beans and dried beef served up cold for lunch; beans and dried beef served for supper—it was enough to break the spirits of the stoutest of men.

Camped two ravines away was Louis, a Basque sheepherder. Over the juniper twig fire a mutton stew simmered in the Dutch oven. The only odor which smelled inviting to Louis was the juniper-scented smoke rising from the fire. The monotonous fare of mutton stew brought no enticing scent at all. As Louis contemplated his culinary fate his experienced ears picked up the sound of the flock working their way northwest. It was time to check the sheep. Supper could wait.

The two buckaroos perked up at the sound of distant bleating and the faint tinkle of the lead ewe's bell. They exchanged glances and each pair of eyes carried the same message—mutton! Their appetites took hold as they sprinted to the top of the ravine. There, not 200 yards away, was a small flock of sheep contentedly nibbling at the dried bunches of grass growing among the sage. No sheepherder or camp was in sight.

Louis walked across the two ravines and along the top of the second, following the sound of the tinkling bell and distant baas. As the flock came into sight he saw them veer to the right at a run! Then he saw a small bunch of twenty-five veer to the left with two men in pursuit. The main flock soon came to a standstill and went back to their grazing. The bunch was divided, twenty rejoining the flock, while five continued running in a wide circle with the two men some distance behind.

Louis would have put an immediate stop to the would-be rustlers had he not caught a whiff of something so fragrant that his taste buds began dancing on the tip of his tongue. He was standing just above a campsite! One glance told Louis that it was a buckaroo camp—which explained why the two men could conceivably believe that they had the ability to run down a fleet-footed sheep. All sheepmen knew that a buckaroo was a sheepherder with his brains knocked out. It would take some time, Louis reasoned, before the buckaroos would realize that they'd never catch the sheep.

Gleefully, Louis swooped down upon the camp and with gloved hand, snatched the Dutch oven from the fire. He hastily made his way back to his camp, the sumptuous fragrance of the beans and beef trailing along behind him.

Louis didn't feel at all sorry that the two hapless rustlers would be without supper, and would have left things that way had his sense of humor not intervened. What if the two buckaroos wearily made their way back to camp after the long, futile chase, eager to sit down to a meal of beans and beef, only to find a Dutch oven full of mutton stew? What a penalty to pay for disturbing his flock, Louis chuckled to himself as he placed the Dutch oven full of mutton stew on the coals of the buckaroo's campfire. What justice!

The Shepherd And Basa Faun

Basa Faun is a gigantic, hairy ogre who lives on human flesh. His feet leave circular imprints on the forest floor as he follows his keen nose in search of prey. The ogre leaps to a large granite boulder outcropping with the agility of a mountain goat to scan the meadow below. There grazes a herd of sheep under the watchful eye of a Basque shepherd.

Instinctively, Basa Faun knows that the shepherd has been careless and does not carry in his pocket a handful of salt crystals as protection against the flesh-eating ogre. Most often Basa Faun would pounce upon the un-suspecting shepherd and devour him at once. Today, the beast decides to give the lad a sporting chance. With several graceful leaps Basa Faun is before the startled shepherd.

"If you state three irrefutable facts," the ogre tells the trembling Basque, "I shall not feast on your flesh, today."

The shepherd thinks a moment, then states, "Some say that when the moon is full, night is as clear as day. That's not true. Some say corn bread is as good as wheat bread. But that's not true. I say, that had I known that you were going to be here I wouldn't have come. And that's true!"

Basa Faun kept his word and bounced back up to his cave. The shepherd never again was without a handful of salt crystals in his pocket.

Basque Moonshine

From 1919 to 1933—the Prohibition years—moonshiners abounded in Jordan Valley, Oregon. Geographically, it was a perfect location. Its remoteness nearly drove government agents crazy trying to cover the area with its isolated cabins located in the midst of dusty, sage-covered flats. It was said that the dust trail following any government vehicle attempting to sneak up on such a place would warn the moonshiner in plenty of time. They not only had time to drink the barrels of "evidence," but time to sober up, as well.

The agent's tasks were compounded by two other factors. One was the attitude of the Jordan Valley residents—sheepmen, buckaroos, and miners—who offered the agents no assistance in tracking down the perpetrators.

The second factor was that a number of Basques had gone from sheep-tending to boot-legging, and, due to their natural craftsmanship abilities, turned out the most sought-after moonshine in the three-corner (Idaho, Oregon, Nevada) region. When caught, these sly moonshiners would resort to their native language—a language, rumor has it, that the devil himself studied for seven years and mastered only two words. Feigning no comprehension of the English language, the red-handed Basques would excitedly speak in Eskuara, using exaggerated hand gestures and pained facial expressions to convey that they knew nothing, understood nothing, and were guilty of nothing. The ploy often frustrated the government agents to such a degree that they'd back off before they were goaded into doing something which may have cost them their jobs.

One prominent Basque citizen of Jordan Valley became one of the most celebrated moonshiners of the area. He had his still hidden in one of the numerous ravines southeast of town. A cold spring ran through the ravine.

He'd make his mash using fifty pounds of beet sugar to one hundred pounds of barley grain. When the mixture began fermentation, he'd transfer it to a large copper kettle hung over a charcoal-fed fire. The heated gas rose up through a copper tube which coiled through a water jacket filled with cold water from the spring. This would cause condensation. A copper tube exiting the water jacket dribbled the alcohol into a jug. The Basque master ran his alcohol to 140 proof, then added distilled spring water to drop it to a drinkable 90 proof.

He'd then filter the whiskey through charcoal. Before pouring the filtered moonshine into the aging barrels, he'd nail a fresh plug of tobacco to the bottom of each keg. The filled barrels were placed in a narrow pool dug from the sandy bottom of the spring. Most of the year the flow of the spring was strong enough to tumble the barrels—movement being an important factor in aging good moonshine.

Once aged, the Basque would load the kegs into the back of a wagon, cover them with sagebrush and transport them to town. Once home, he'd add the sage to his winter woodpile and a pick-up man would relieve him of the kegs.

The pick-up man took the risk of being caught transporting the moonshine to Caldwell, Vale, and sometimes LaGrande, for the sum of three dollars per gallon.

However, it became more and more risky to travel the public roads which had become well-patrolled. Authorities were bravely attempting to staunch the flow of illegal booze from the Jordan Valley area. The pick-up man began demanding four dollars per gallon delivery charge due to the increased risk.

Though the Basque's whiskey cost approximately one dollar per gallon to manufacture, and sold for fifteen dollars per gallon due to its exceptional quality, it seemed extravagant to pay the pick-up man four bucks just to deliver the stuff. When an unusually large order came in from LaGrande, the enterprising Basque decided to deliver it himself.

At midday, he began his run. About ten miles into his journey a black cat darted across the road. Being a man who didn't take such signs lightly, he left the main road and took a steep, winding route along an ill-kept graveled back road. It took him three times as long to reach his destination, and he feared that perhaps his clients had figured that he'd been caught and made their purchases elsewhere. This, however, was not the case. The tavern owners were elated to see him! The town was nearly dry. A roadblock five miles south of LaGrande had netted all the moonshine coming into the area. All, that is, but the moonshine carried by one superstitious Basque moonshiner.

A Matter Of Honor

"Old Sunday" worked as a herder for a man named McEwen. The Basque herder was a quiet man who enjoyed his solitude. Never-the-less, on one sweltering August afternoon, "Old Sunday" felt a stir of excitement as he watched the dust trail across the flat, sage-covered landscape. He had been nearly a month without a visitor.

As the camptender pulled the dusty mules and canvas-covered wagon to a halt before "Old Sunday's" tent he spied the herder sawing some mutton chops from the carcass of a freshly dressed ewe with a somewhat rusty meat saw. Now, the camptender was a fellow Basque with whom "Old Sunday" frequently quarreled, and he wasn't about to allow an opportunity to pass him by. Without polite salutation, the camptender made the observation that, due to its apparent dullness, the saw was doing a good job of turning a fine side of chops into ground mutton.

To this, "Old Sunday" replied that the saw was sharp enough to cut through the barrel of a rifle.

Thus the two Basques spent the evening arguing over the abilities of the meat saw. When the camptender retired to his bedroll, he left the argument dangling in the warm, sage-scented air. The frustrated herder took to his tent.

A .44-.40 Winchester rifle was propped against one of the flat-sided walls of the canvas tent. It belonged to McEwen, "Old Sunday's" boss, and it was to be used in any emergency which may befall the herder or his flock.

It didn't take long for "Old Sunday" to decide that his honor was at stake and that the situation could thus be deemed as an emergency situation. The herder stayed up all night feverishly sawing away at the barrel of the Winchester.

Both the rifle and the meat saw were ruined, but "Old Sunday" had a few moments of glory early the next morning as he waved the sawed off barrel in the face of the startled camptender.

"Experienced" Herders

Jose had come to Nevada from his homeland in "Euzkadi" the fall of 1922. He felt extremely fortunate. An uncle had immigrated to Nevada in 1915. After five and one half years of herding sheep, the uncle had accumulated enough money to purchase a hotel in Winnemucca. With his contacts in the sheep business, Jose's uncle was able to secure a job for his nephew.

Since an immigration quota system had been put into effect in 1921, it had become extremely difficult for Basques, as well as others from foreign lands, to enter the United States. However, there remained a shortage of sheepherders, so wool growers put a good deal of pressure on Congress. A bill, spearheaded by Idaho and Nevada congressmen, was passed. It was to "provide relief for the sheep industry by making special quota immigration visas available to certain alien sheepherders."

Jose and Alejo, another Basque fresh from the Old Country, were to trail a flock over a relatively low mountain range to winter pasture. As they headed off with the 750 woolly animals, each was confident in the other's abilities. The sheep contentedly meandered along the mountain trail and when evening came, formed a loose bunch among the scrub brush growing amid a mountain meadow.

The two men were weary, but content. Each felt that he was in the company of an experienced herder. Everything had gone so smoothly that first day.

The following morning, however, shattered whatever confidence each had in the other. An early snowstorm had heavily blanketed the mountain. The two men burrowed out of their camp tent and looked out across the white landscape. Pillows of snow covered the scrub brush. Not a sheep was in sight!

"Where are the sheep!" shouted Jose, in Basque.

to seek the safety of the store, so lacking the heart to turn the hysterical man away, the Barbers allowed him to stay the night. The Basque was still quite shaken the following morning. Charles Barber and another man went with the Basque to his sheep camp. It was then a simple matter to piece together the details of the ghost story.

The night before, the Basque had done his laundry and hung it on a line stretched between two trees to dry. The men speculated that "Russian John," a local part-time forest ranger, had come along on horseback late at night—most likely returning from one of his drinking bouts—and had gotten himself tangled up in the laundry. The horse spooked and went racing through the night with the screaming, laundry-draped Russian clinging to its back.

Itzala

The abandoned Army training base near Kettleman Hills, southwest of Fresno, California, was the home of a canine believed to be half-coyote and half-German shepherd.

The Basques pasturing sheep in the Kettleman Hills named the canine Itzala, meaning Shadow, for she stealthily moved about at night picking off prime lambs. She seemed to make a game of eluding the sheepmen, appearing in plain sight when none had a gun at hand or peering around the corner of some abandoned barracks and pulling her lips back over her teeth in what appeared to be a wicked grin.

The sheepmen were determined to bring about her demise, especially a Basque named Maness Etcheverry. She had become his vendetta. On one occasion, Itzala was spotted in open pasture. Several Basques, Maness included, piled into a pickup and took after her. She leaped and dodged through sagebrush clumps as bullets whizzed over her head and drew puffs of dust to her left and right. Then down into a draw she went, the pickup in hot pursuit, but Itzala bounded up and out, while the pickup wobbled to a halt on busted springs.

Then twenty traps were set along a narrow bridge. Itzala danced around them with grace. Her dainty tracks were clearly visible in the soft dirt.

The next tactic which the Basques devised was to drive her from the abandoned barracks and shoot her as she fled. For four hours six men went from one building to the next shaking tin cans filled with stones. Finally Maness Etcheverry spied her as she disappeared into an old warehouse. He and a friend entered the building and spotted her in the corner of a tool storage area that had a half-door entrance. At her feet were two tiny pups. Maness aimed his rifle at her but before he could get a clear shot, she jumped out the half-door, nearly knocking

Meanwhile, the bogged cattle had struggled to solid ground. The mired horses, not wanting to be left behind, managed to wallow through the sucking mire after them. Though the exhausted, shaking horses would have preferred to stand and blow wind awhile, their anxious riders spurred them up the ravine to see what had become of Buckaroo Joe. They joined a number of other Basque cowboys who had gathered to peer over the edge and speculate.

"Did you see the look on Joe's face as he went over?" one said. "It was a look of complete surprise. Like falling into that hole wasn't an option. Like that pinto was just going to keep sailing on."

Way down in the ravine the belly of the prostrate pinto could be seen. There was no sign of Buckaroo Joe, presumed dead in the saddle beneath the horse.

"He was a good rider. But not as good as he thought himself to be," another said, shaking his head in disbelief. "Damn fool thing he did this time."

"Killed himself and a darn good cow horse, too," said yet another Basque cowboy. "Going to miss him though. Good cow boss."

"How do we get Joe out?" asked the Basque greenhorn.

"Why try?" someone said. "He must be dead. We push in the bank and bury him here."

After a brief discussion among the cowboys it was agreed that that idea made the best sense.

The pinto suddenly heaved upright, and with great

effort, crawled up the steep-sided gully. Clawing up behind was Buckaroo Joe, blood streaming from his broken nose and a dislocated finger sticking up at an odd angle. He turned to the men and said, "I heard you! You don't bury me today! Not in this ditch. Catch me my horse."

With that, he climbed up on the pinto, mopped blood off his face, tugged at his dislocated finger, and proceeded with the cattle drive.

Antonio And The Priest

Antonio, a widower, was a teller of tales and a singer of songs. His company was appreciated and solicited by many. Antonio's young son, Manuel, was usually asked to accompany his father when Antonio was invited to dine with a family or to entertain.

One day the local priest was expecting special out-of-town guests and thought that it would be pleasant to invite Antonio to dine at his table and sing some songs. The priest's invitation, however, didn't include Manuel. Antonio told Manuel not to fret, for a free meal would be his, as well. Manuel was instructed to wait outside the priest's house by the front door.

When all the guests had been seated at the priest's table, Antonio announced that he would like the honor of saying grace. The priest gave an approving nod. Antonio said grace and concluded, "In the name of the Father and the Holy Ghost." All eyes turned to Antonio. The priest cleared his throat, then said, "Antonio, have you forgotten 'the Son'?" "Of course not," Antonio exclaimed, jumping up. "He's outside! I'll bring him at once."

The Kapatseko-Denbora Feast

A journalist frequented a Basque restaurant in Ontario, Oregon, and eventually established friendships with several sheepmen who were also regulars. He so often praised the Basque cuisine that one of the herders invited him to attend an upcoming kapatseko-denbora feast being held at one of the sheep corrals.

The journalist eagerly accepted. He not only anticipated the offer of authentic cuisine, but the opportunity to learn more about the elusive Basque, as well. Dressed in denims, cowboy boots, and red bandanna, the journalist arrived at the corrals determined to fit in with his new friends. He was surprised to see about a dozen Basques busily castrating, docking, and branding lambs. With a casual air he strolled up to his friend and offered his assistance. He was directed to the castrating pens. There he observed the procedure.

While one Basque held a lamb by its hind hooves, another made a slice at the end of the scrotum and extracted the testicles. The Basque then grasped the testicles between his teeth and with one smooth pull of his head, detached the orbs from the lamb. The testicles were spat into a bucket. The Basque then shot a stream of wine into his mouth from a leather bag and gargled before proceeding with the next lamb. Though it was explained to the journalist that this was the safest method of castrating for the lamb, the display was too much for the man. He took his queasy stomach to the next corral where the tail docking was taking place. Seeing the tails hacked from the squirming lambs caused further discomfort. The sight of several pails filled with lambless tails was also disquieting, so the journalist went on to the branding pen.

Here he found his temporary vocation. For the remainder of the day the journalist dipped a wooden brand into warm black dye and stamped the backs of the lambs. By day's end he was famished.

A wonderful aroma rose from the Dutch ovens positioned over the campfire. Loaves of sourdough bread cooled nearby. Hungrily the journalist took his place in line, plate in hand, but his appetite took a turn when he peered into the Dutch oven and saw that kapatsekodenbora was lamb testicles and tails browned in garlic-flavored olive oil.

Juan Jose's Laminak

Juan Jose tended a small flock of sheep in the Pyrenees for his father. The boy dreamed of going to the United States as the herder of a large band as his uncle had, but he lacked self-trust.

Every day, while tending the flock, Juan Jose would look beneath fallen tree limbs and into rock crevices searching for the legendary Laminak. Laminak was a small dwarf sheep mascot. With the mascot as his lucky charm, combined with his own ability to work hard, Juan Jose knew that he could be a success as a herder in the new country.

The day came when Juan Jose received word from his uncle. The missive asked Juan Jose to come to his uncle's ranch in Oregon and work as a herder. The proposition both troubled and excited the boy. Was he capable of going to a new country and tending ten times the number of sheep he currently managed? How could he not seize this great opportunity? With the money his uncle had sent he booked passage on the next ship preparing to sail.

During the week before his scheduled departure Juan Jose combed the forest for Laminak. The day before he was due to leave he came upon a small cave beneath a spreading oak. Juan Jose had to wiggle into the cave on his belly. As he wiggled through the passage he came to a small compartment with barely enough room to stand. The floor was covered with soft leaf mold. A bed of cushion-like green moss lay in one corner. Juan Jose knew that this must be the cave of the coveted Laminak, so he hid behind a broad pillar of stone and waited.

Before long he heard something coming through the passage. It was making a grumbling noise which sounded like a low pitched "naggity, naggity, naggity." Perhaps Laminak, reputed to be a cheerful dwarf, had a bad day. When the critter came into sight, Juan Jose was

A Matter Of Intelligence

It was February 5, Zanta Agueda's Day. To honor the saint, several Jordan Valley Basque men gathered to celebrate. In Old World tradition the men went from house to house singing to Saint Zanta Agueda, keeping time with a wooden stick. At the houses visited they were given chorizos, bacon, cubed lamb, and other treats to make up the feast to be held at the end of their visiting. Some houses even offered glassfuls of strong drink.

As they moved from house to house, more and more Basques joined the march and the singing. The group ended up at the Marquina, a Basque hotel, where the treats gathered would be prepared for the feast. There, the men continued drinking while a group of Basque women worked at setting the tables with food.

However, the gaiety turned sour when the men launched into an argument over which were the smarter—buckaroos or sheepherders. Many of the men who had originally herded sheep and had since become buckaroos sided against the sheepherders. The argument became louder and more aggressive. There seemed to be no way to resolve the argument.

No longer able to hold her tongue, one elderly Basque woman stepped up to the bickering group. She grabbed the wooden stick the men had used to keep time during their singing and loudly tapped it on the table. The room grew silent.

"This I tell you," she said with quiet dignity, "when my husband came to this country he wished to be a buckaroo, but buckaroos were only earning twenty-five dollars a month. Now, sheepherders, they got thirty dollars. He went for the money. Now, tell me who's the smarter?"

Idaho's Oinkari Basque Dancers

The love of dancing was not left behind in the Basque homeland of "Euzkadi" when men and women emigrated to the United States. The Victory Dance, the Wine Glass Dance, and the Jota were just a few of the lively dances which echoed through such boarding houses as Idaho's Star Rooming House, Hotel Iberia, and the De Lamar Hotel. Similar dancing bowed the hardwood floors of California's Yturri Hotel and Basque Hotel. They rattled the windows of Nevada's Telescope, Star, and Overland boarding houses. Wherever the Basques went in their new country, they brought their spirited dances with them.

In 1960, a group of seven Idaho dancers visited San Sebastian. There, in the native land of their ancestors, they watched a group of dancers on the street. The San Sebastian dancers called their group the Oinkari, meaning "to do with feet." The Boise dancers were enthralled with some of the dances performed by this group— among them the Auku (hoop dance) and the Ikurrina (the fallen warrior). Soon the Idaho dancers were dancing several times a week with the Oinkari group, learning the new steps.

When they left San Sebastian, the Idaho dancers vowed to begin their own group in the United States called *Oinkari,* in honor of the San Sebastian dancers.

In 1964 the Oinkari Basque dancers were a main attraction for Idaho Day at New York's World Fair. Since they were already back east, Idaho's Senators Frank Church and Len Jordan arranged for them to perform in Washington, D.C. at the Rotunda of the Senate Office Building.

In their quiet and stately manner the Oinkari Dancers entered the Rotunda. A small, polite audience was seated, awaiting the performance. Masses of people mingled in the hallways of the building amusing themselves with the typical political chatter. A dancer stepped forth and gave the irrintzi—the traditional Basque warrior cry—the signal to begin the performance.

All doors leading to the Rotunda sprang open as hordes of people streamed in to see what had caused the hair-raising shriek. They were treated to lively Basque dances performed by dancers in colorful costumes who circled, swung, and broke to the rhythm of accordions and tambourines.

The Sheepman And The BLM Man

When the Basques moved into the Jordan Valley area, grazing was not controlled. Aside from a few established ranches, range land was open to free grazing. As more and more livestock—sheep, cattle, and horses—came into the area, the open range became so over-grazed that the land turned desert-like.

The established ranchers resented the destruction caused by rawhiders (cattlemen who moved their cattle from one range to another) and sheep tramps, who operated in the same manner as the rawhiders.

The passage of the Taylor Grazing Act of 1934 made such grazing illegal. Under the act, all users were required to show proof of a base of operations. Priorities were also established, granting seniority to the old-timers of the range.

The Bureau of Land Management established the rules and regulations regarding the use of the land. The majority of the newly appointed range managers were former cattlemen and sheepmen who had failed to be successful in their chosen professions. Many misused their power, acting as Lords of the Land and never bending from the "rules of the book." The ranchers resented being bossed around by those whom they felt were less than their peers—men who traded in their worn work boots to walk in the soft, new shoes of government employees.

The bad impressions made by the earlier land managers were very difficult for later managers to overcome. A new manager was eager to make a good impression on the land users of the Jordan Valley area. He wanted the people to know that he was working for them, not against them.

One particular Basque sheep rancher had had a difficult time with the BLM men for years and was not encouraged by the appearance of the new area manager. However, the new manager was determined to win the confidence of the crusty old-timer. He sat down with the Basque sheep rancher and, over a cup of coffee, explained that the two of them would have no difficulty talking things over and working things out. He had, after all, an "open door policy."

To this, the Basque retorted, "The door he have nothing to do with it. You all read out of the same book."

Bear-Dog Boy

Philippe's mother had been reluctant to allow her ten-year-old son to spend the month of July in a Stanley Basin sheep camp with his father. She knew the rigors of camp life and was concerned that her husband may not have had the time necessary to see to the needs of their son. However, her husband had convinced her that the boy could come to no harm.

The excited Philippe rode to his father's camp with the camp tender, a Swede named Joe. The smell of the hot July landscape—a mingling of pungent sage and woodsy lodgepole pine—filled his nostrils. The clackity-clack-clack of grasshoppers filled his ears. The joy of adventure filled his heart, even though he had no idea what that adventure might be. His ten-year-old intuition told him that he would find a good one.

His father had supper ready when they reached camp. A plump sage hen simmered in a thick gravy in the Dutch oven, along with chunks of new potatoes. After the tin plates were rinsed and put away, Philippe, his father, and the two sheep dogs hiked over the knoll to check the sheep. Even to his inexperienced eyes, Philippe could see that the sheep were in distress. They were bunched up and leaping on each other's backs.

"There!" his father said. "A black bear."

At that moment the two dogs took off after the bear. The animal lumbered over to a stand of lodgepole and scaled up one of the spindly trees. While the dogs kept it at bay, Philippe's father approached the tree with the boy scampering along behind.

Looking up at the bear, Philippe's father stated, "The hide's worth five dollars. That's two and a half day's wages. Joe's got a .22 in the wagon. Philippe, stay here with the dogs. I'll be right back."

As Philippe stepped closer to get a clearer view of the bear, his father jogged off in the direction of camp. The man was confident that the dogs would keep the bear in its place until he returned. The dogs, however, lost the excitement of the moment and looked around for their master. Finding him gone, they took off in pursuit.

Philippe stood at the base of the tree staring up at the bear. The bear sized up the boy and determined that he was little threat. Slowly the bear began backing down the tree.

"Bear! Git back up there, bear!" Philippe yelled. He grabbed a stick and banged the base of the tree. Growling softly to himself, the bear inched back up the tree.

Every few minutes the bear would test the boy and try to back down the tree. Philippe was determined not to lose his father's bear and managed to bluff the animal back up the tree.

Finally Philippe's father crested the knoll and headed down with the dogs and the .22. The camp tender, Joe, appeared at the top of the knoll and watched the event.

Seeing that he had an audience, Philippe danced around the base of the tree and barked up at the bear. He made quite a show of it. The bear, becoming aggravated with the antics of the boy, growled aggressively.

It took Philippe's father three shots from the .22 to kill the bear. He skinned the animal and packed the hide back to camp. Joe had little to say about the bear escapade until Philippe was sound asleep in his bed roll. Only then did he approach the father.

"Basco," he said, "that boy won't last the month if you continue to use him as a bear-dog."

Sunday At The "Nat"

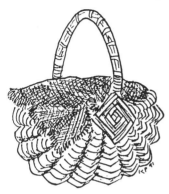

Louee met and fell in love with Leandra in the Old Country, but felt that he had little to offer the green-eyed, light-hearted girl in the way of security. In 1920, when he had the opportunity to come to Idaho to work at a limestone quarry with his brother, Fidel, he left Leandra behind. He made no promises to her, for he was uncertain how he would fare in Idaho. Leandra waited.

Three years later, with a secure future before him, Louee sent for Leandra. On a July afternoon, with a mixture of excitement and apprehension, they reunited at the Boise train depot. Leandra had grown to womanhood. Though her beauty and poise took Louee's breath away, he felt strange at their reunion. This was not the laughing, playful Leandra he had remembered. Nor did Leandra find Louee the carefree, funfilled lad she had bid farewell to three years earlier.

Leandra stayed with friends of her mother's sister on Broadway Street. Louee stayed at Mateo Arrequiri's De Lamar Hotel, a Basque boarding house. Each evening, after work at the quarry, Louee would walk the short distance from the boarding house to Broadway to take Leandra to dinner or a picture show. They would ride the trolley to their destination. After two weeks of dating, their relationship remained strained.

Then one Sunday, after they had attended services at St. John's Cathedral, Louee decided to take Leandra to Boise's Natatorium Amusement Park. He packed a picnic lunch.

When their trolley pulled up to Trolley Inn, Louee and Leandra stepped off and strolled through the park's rose garden. The Natatorium loomed before them, its two six-story-high towers standing stark white against the robin's egg sky. Leandra's eyes shone with excitement as they passed through the arched doorway to view the gigantic spring heated pool. Water spouted from a large sand-stone fountain. Stairs led up to four open galleries that looked down over the pool, but Leandra did not want to view the fun, she wanted to be in the center of it!

After their swim, the couple took the half-mile trip on the scenic railway. This was followed by an adventurous ride on the joy-wheel. The centrifugal force of the joy-wheel threw the couple against the padded sides where they clung to each other, laughing uncontrollably. They would rest on the grass until their dizziness passed, then climb up the wooden steps to the dish-shaped joy-wheel for another go-around. Finally, the popcorn-scented air reminded them of their uneaten picnic, so they settled in a cool, shady portion of the lawn and ate.

Music from the bandstand filled the air as they relaxed into friendly talk. Then, hand in hand, they wandered the grounds exploring the fun house with its crazy mirrors, and trying their luck at the shooting gallery. They watched the skaters at the roller rink. As the sun waned, the skating rink turned into a dance hall. The evening found Louee and Leandra dancing Jota-like steps to the snappy tunes of the contemporary band. Other Basques joined them in dance, and soon the entire crowd, including a couple of Chinese, were imitating the steps. The members of the band caught on to the mood of the group and did all in their power to match their beat to the wild pace of the dancers.

That evening, at the Natatorium, Louee and Leandra set their wedding date. In the years which followed, the couple made Sunday at the "Nat" a tradition—something shared with their two children.

Fourteen years later the tradition was halted. In 1934, a raging windstorm swept through the Boise Valley and the

Natatorium was destroyed. Since the tragedy took place during the Depression, no funds were available to make repairs. The grand amusement park, however, lived in the memories of many who shared in its magic.

The Grandmother And The Shepherd

The Grandmother lived near Los Angeles, California. She had been born and raised in Chicago, so she had always been a city inhabitant. The Grandmother dressed in the latest styles and her impeccable manners would have impressed Emily Post.

Visiting her daughter and grandchildren in Idaho was like going on safari. The small mountain village known as McCall seemed as remote a region as the Grandmother was likely to experience.

It wasn't the wild beasts and bugs which frequented the mountain town that distressed the Grandmother—it was the condition of her only granddaughter which she found appalling. The girl dressed in jeans and T-shirts, and rode upon the bare back of a dusty burro. The girl spent a great deal of time in the woods. Alone! That concerned the Grandmother.

She fretted over the child's safety. Since danger in the city often lurked in the form of "strange men," the Grandmother felt the need to caution the granddaughter against talking to strange men who may be lurking in the woods.

"But Grandma," the child said, "there are no strange men in the woods to talk to. The only men I talk to are in the meadows herding the sheep."

"There are shepherds there?" Mused the Grandmother. "You will be safe among the shepherds."

The shepherds the Grandmother envisioned were the Biblical type with long flowing robes and curved hardwood staffs, their clean, Christ-like hair hanging gracefully across their shoulders.

In reality, the men who herded the sheep were Basque. They stayed in camp week in and week out with a handful of dogs and a couple of mules for companionship. They "bathed" in a tin of water heated over the open campfire. There was no dress code among the sheep camps. The only certainty was that the men wore the same scent—essence of sheep.

The Grandmother was correct on one account. Her granddaughter would be safe among the "shepherds."

Once when the burro got tangled in discarded barbed-wire, a Basque sheepherder appeared from the timber, untangled the frantic animal and wiped the tears from the little girl's face with his soiled red bandanna. He vanished back into the timber as quickly as he had come.

Another time a Basque herder saw the burro, in an ornery mood, dump the girl in the trail and high-tail it towards home. The Basque captured the fleeing burro and returned it to the humiliated girl. Not once did he crack a smile as the girl scolded the errant burro. Instead

he stood solemnly aside until the girl calmed down enough to mount the burro and ride away.

One day the girl spotted a black lamb among a band of sheep and, in her desire to have the lamb, forgot her alliance with the herders as well as lessons of right and wrong. With the aid of her dog she scattered the band and managed to corner the lamb. She brought it home slung over the back of the burro. Her father made a straw bed in one of the barn stables for the "found" lamb.

The Basque are known for their tenacity in caring for the sheep. The herder of the band tracked the burro which led to the house where the girl lived.

It was a misfortune that the Grandmother was visiting at that time and was the one to answer the knock on the door. The ragged, sheep-scented man standing in the doorway was, to the Grandmother, a nightmarish vision of the classic "strange man." She stood pale and trembling as the man, speaking in broken English, attempted to explain the circumstances of the stolen lamb. Slowly it became clear to the Grandmother that this man was a "shepherd from the meadows."

Selected Bibliography

Andy Little, Idaho Sheep King. Louise Shadduck; Caxton Printers, 1990.

The Basques—Preservation of a Culture. Lynne Fereday; Lynne Fereday Scholarship Memorial, 1971.

Basques From the Pyrenees to the Rockies. Bernice Brusen; Utah, 1985.

Beckoning the Bold. Rafe Gibbs; University Press of Idaho, 1976.

Beltron—Basque Sheepman of the American West. Beltron Paris; University of Nevada Press, 1979.

The Book of the Basques. Rodney Gallop; University of Nevada Press, 1970.

Harney County Oregon. George Francis Brimlow; Maverick Publications, 1980.

Idaho Folklore—Homesteads to Headstones. Louie W. Attebery; University of Utah Press, 1985.

The Idaho Heritage. Edited by Richard W. Etulain and Bert W. Marley; Idaho State University Press, 1974.

Idaho's Place in the Sun. Helen M. Newell; Syms-York, 1975.

Owyhee Trails, The West's Forgotten Corner. Mike Hanley and Ellis Lucia; Caxton Printers, 1988.

Sawtooth Tales. Dick d Easum; Caxton Printers, 1980.

75 Years of Memories. Henry Alegria; Alegria, 1981.

A Shepherd Watches, A Shepherd Sings. Louis Irigaray and Theodore Taylor; Doubleday, 1977.

Stanley-Sawtooth Country. Esther Yarber; Publishers Press, 1976.

Tales of the I.O.N. Country. Mike Hanley; Hanley, 1988.

Traditional Basque Cooking—History and Preparation. Jose' Maria Busca Isusi; University of Nevada Press, 1987.

The Witche's Advocate. Gustari Henningsen; University of Nevada Press, 1980.

Periodical:

Nevada Hiways and Parks. Fall, 1966.

Lamb Sources

To find out where lamb is available in any given area contact:

American Lamb Council
Denver Office
200 Clayton
Denver, CO 80206
(303) 399-8130

Lamb available for shipping:

Gem Meat Packing Company
515 East 45th
Garden City, ID
(208) 375-9424

Recipe Index

Lore Index